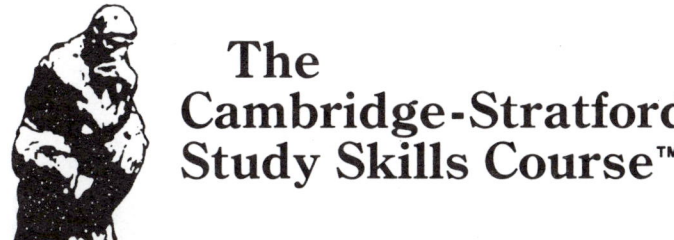

The Cambridge-Stratford Study Skills Course™

division of Cambridge Stratford, Ltd.

Notes:

A College Study Skills Manual
Ten Tips for Academic Success

Student's Text and Workbook

June Crawford
Niagara University

Typeset By: YG Yearke Graphics

TO THE STUDENT

Have you ever wondered what learning would be like if you fully realized your academic potential? That means *being as successful as you are capable of being* by "stretching your mind" and operating on "all cylinders." "Oh no," you sigh inwardly. "I've never been a bookworm and I don't want to be one!" STOP sighing and groaning and read on for *good news*. The Cambridge-Stratford Study Skills Course is about making your study time more efficient, NOT making you study for more time. The Cambridge-Stratford Study Skills Course will help you USE and APPLY learning skills and study techniques with which you are already familiar; you will become an expert in LEARNING HOW TO LEARN! What's the magic formula? It's *YOU*, and a willingness to utilize basic psychological factors of learning in your daily academic life. You will need the determination to break old habits and to form new ones. You will need to attend class regularly, have an open mind and a desire to be successful.

The staff of the Cambridge-Stratford Study Skills Institute wishes you success in what could be the most important and valuable hours of your academic life!

Notes:

ABOUT THE AUTHOR

June Justice Crawford, Ed.M.

Mrs. Crawford is the director of the Learning Center at Niagara University in Niagara Falls, New York. Under her direction, Niagara's Learning Center has been named an "Exemplary Program" in the United States by the Center for Developmental Education, which is located at Appalachian State University, Boone, North Carolina. Mrs. Crawford is a reading specialist who has taught reading, study skills and English at several colleges and universities in the Western New York area. In addition, she has served as a consultant to a number of colleges and has taught classes to improve reading skills for private industries in her area. Mrs. Crawford is a doctoral candidate in Research and Evaluation at the State University of New York at Buffalo. She also holds an associate's degree in liberal arts, a bachelor's degree in English, and a master's degree in reading from SUNYAB.

ABOUT THE PUBLISHER

The CAMBRIDGE-STRATFORD STUDY SKILLS INSTITUTE is an international organization of professionals dedicated to the pursuit of helping students of all ages LEARN BETTER, READ FASTER and SCORE HIGHER on TESTS, key ingredients for success in school as well as in life.

As a division of Cambridge-Stratford, Ltd., the INSTITUTE provides in-service training and consulting to teaching staff plus formal instruction for students in the middle school through college levels using the nationally renowned editions of the Cambridge-Stratford Study Skills Course (10 hour, 20 hour, 30 hour: grades 6-13).

Copyright © 1988 by Cambridge Stratford, Limited. All rights reserved. No part of this work may be reproduced or transmitted in any form or by any means, electronic or mechanical, including photocopying and recording, or by any information storage or retrieval system, except as may be expressly permitted by the 1976 Copyright Act or in writing by the Publisher. Requests for permission should be addressed in writing to Permissions Department, Cambridge-Stratford, Ltd., 8560 Main Street, Williamsville, New York 14221.

Printed in the USA.

ISBN: 0-935637-12-5

4th Printing © 1995

Table of Contents

LESSON 1	GOAL SETTING What Am I Doing Here Anyway?	1
LESSON 2	TIME MANAGEMENT Time Flies When You Are Having Fun	9
LESSON 3	CRITICAL THINKING/PROBLEM SOLVING Thinking Caps In Place Now: Let's Try It!	21
LESSON 4	MEMORIZATION Elephants Never Forget: How About You?	33
LESSON 5	SPEED READING Reading Rates For College: Life In The Fast Lane	39
LESSON 6	READING FOR COMPREHENSION Reading For Learning: Slow Me Down, Lord!	67
LESSON 7	VOCABULARY BUILDING Words, Words, Words: Where's The Action?	81
LESSON 8	LISTENING SKILLS I Can't Hear You: I've Got My Headphones On	89
LESSON 9	NOTE TAKING/OUTLINING Music To Your Ears: Lecture Notes	95
LESSON 10	TEST TAKING You Want Me To Do What? Take A Test?	105

Cambridge-Stratford Study Skills Course
Ten Hour College Course

Lesson Objectives

Lesson 1

1. The student should be able to identify his/her study skill strengths and weaknesses and determine which areas require improvement.
2. The student will be able to verbalize at least three reasons for enrolling at the college.
3. The student will identify his/her strongest and weakest learning mode and be able to explain one activity which can be engaged in to overcome the weakness.
4. The student will establish a minimum of three goals for the college semester and list at least one objective for each of the goals which he/she plans to accomplish within the next week.

Lesson 2

1. The student will recognize the importance of efficient use of time.
2. The student should be able to plan the amount of time he/she should spend in study each week.
3. The student will produce a weekly schedule to be used as a guide for one semester.
4. The student should be able to relate the planning for one semester to the need for a weekly schedule for use of study time.

Lesson 3

1. The student will demonstrate a knowledge of the differences among literal, inferential, critical and analytical thinking.
2. The student should be able to demonstrate the ability to use different thinking skills for different tasks as he/she studies.
3. Given a problem, the student should be able to list the steps which must be taken to solve the problem.
4. The student will be able to give an example of convergent thinking and an example of divergent thinking and explain the difference.

Lesson 4

1. The student should be able to distinguish between short- and long-term memory.
2. The student will be able to define the concepts of motivation, selectivity, clarification, association and review in memorizing and studying material.
3. The student will be able to give an example of a subject which could be studied which would utilize the magic number seven method of memory.
4. The student will be able to define and give at least two examples of mnemonic devices and relate their use to college study.

Lesson 5

1. The student will recognize at least three different reading rates to be used for three different purposes in college reading tasks.
2. The student should be able to determine his/her own current reading rate.
3. The student will establish a goal and a personal plan to double his/her reading rate within a four week period.

Lesson Objectives

Lesson 6

1. The student will recognize the need for several steps in reading a textbook for study purposes.

2. The student will be able to establish the optimum reading rate for study purposes.

3. The student will be able to state the steps used in the SQ3R Reading Method.

Lesson 7

1. The student should be able to recognize the importance of vocabulary development for improved reading ability and the understanding of new concepts in college classes.

2. The student will be able to state at least five methods of learning new vocabulary.

3. The student should be able to identify the roots and affixes most frequently used in English words.

4. The student should be able to recognize the twenty words least apt to be known by college freshmen but most often used in college textbooks.

Lesson 8

1. The student will be able to recognize the difference between hearing a noise and actually listening to a sound.

2. The student will demonstrate the ability to listen and repeat information which is given by classmates.

3. Given a specific piece of knowledge, the student will be able to share this information with the class, and listen to make a decision about how the information relates to other facts presented by classmates.

Lesson 9

1. The student should exhibit the ability to produce two pages of clear, neat, useful notes for study.

2. The student should be able to list at least five direction words which guide our listening.

3. The student should be able to take notes using the method taught, and be able to produce study materials from the notes.

Lesson 10

1. The student should be able to recognize at least five different types of test questions which may appear on college exams.

2. The student will determine how to maximize his/her chances of choosing the correct answer on a multiple choice exam.

3. The student should be able to recognize the differences among terms used in essay questions on an exam, and determine how to answer the question.

NOTES

Bibliography

Albanese, Jay S. <u>Dealing With Delinquency</u>. New York: University Press of America, Inc., 1985; pages 40-45.

Bennett, William. "Love Of Learning Still Has A Place In College Life," <u>U.S. News & World Report</u>. November 25, 1985; page 37.

Findsen, Owen. "Some Leaders Are Born Women," Gannett News Service, March 23, 1986; page 11.

Freeman, Don. "Baseball Dreams," <u>Saturday Review</u>. May/June 1985; pages 15-16.

"How Much Sleep Is Enough," <u>Psychology Today</u>. June, 1986; page 45.

Krajick, Kevin. "Do Seat Belts Kill," <u>Psychology Today</u>. May, 1986; pages 10-11.

McGlen, Nancy E. and O'Connor, Karen. "Women's Rights: The Struggle For Equality In The 19th & 20th Century," a lecture adapted from: <u>Women's Rights</u>. New York: Praeger Publishers, Inc., 1983.

Parker, Dorothy. "Observation," <u>The Portable Dorothy Parker</u>. New York: Viking Penquin, Inc., 1954, page 112.

Parker, Dorothy. "Philosophy," <u>The Portable Dorothy Parker</u>. New York: Viking Penquin, Inc., 1954, page 107.

Parker, Dorothy. "The Flaw In Paganism," <u>The Portable Dorothy Parker</u>. New York: Viking Penquin, Inc., 1956, page 298.

Pillitteri, Adele. <u>Maternal Newborn Nursing: Care Of The Growing Family</u>. 2nd Edition; Boston: Little, Brown and Company, Inc., 1981, pages 45-52.

Potter, Robert R. "Victor The Wolf Boy," <u>English Everywhere: Meaning, Media and You</u>. New York: Globe Book Company, 1971; page 14.

Stanford, Gene and Dobbs, Barbara. "Mystery Of The Bank Robbery," <u>Learning Discussion Skills Through Games</u>. New York; Scholastic, Inc., 1975; page 82.

© 1988 by Cambridge Stratford, LTD.

Goal Setting

Lesson 1
WHAT AM I DOING HERE ANYWAY?

Objectives

1. The student should be able to identify his/her study skill strengths and weaknesses and determine which areas require improvement.

2. The student will be able to verbalize at least three reasons for enrolling at the college.

3. The student will identify his/her strongest and weakest learning mode and be able to explain one activity which can be engaged in to overcome the weakness.

4. The student will establish a minimum of three goals for the college semester and list at least one objective for each of the goals which he/she plans to accomplish within the next week.

Notes

PRE-TEST
Test Your Knowledge of College Study Skills

1. There are _____ major ways in which people learn.

2. The rule-of-thumb for number of study hours per week is _____ hours out of class for every hour in class.

3. On a four point scale, if a person gets a grade of "B" in a three-hour course, there are _____ quality points added to his college average.

4. The average reading speed of an American is _____ words per minute.

5. Good college readers utilize at least _____ rates of reading.

6. In the study method SQ3R, the last R stands for _____ .

7. Forty-eight hours after hearing a lecture, a person who does not take notes remembers less than _____ percent of the material.

8. Which of the following is an example of a mnemonic device:
   a. arithmetic times tables
   b. "30 days hath September..."
   c. motivation
   d. computer drills

9. Roots and affixes are useful in the study of:
   a. vocabulary words
   b. plants and spiders
   c. cultural backgrounds
   d. clearing out trees

10. Only about _____ percent of the students who enter college actually finish a degree program.

11. There are at least _____ methods for learning new words from college textbooks and lectures.

12. Some of the first things a student should do when reading a textbook chapter are
    a. read the introduction and summary
    b. look at the pictures, charts, graphs, etc.
    c. count the pages and estimate how long it will take to read
    d. all of the above

13. The narrow column on notepaper should be used for _____ .

14. Note taking should be done on only one side of a sheet of paper.
    _____ True   _____ False

15. Reading and listening are two ways we learn. Another way is to actually _____ something.

Lesson 1: WHAT AM I DOING HERE ANYWAY?

Notes

16. In taking lecture notes, you should record the examples an instructor gives in the lecture.
    _____ True   _____ False

17. There are at least _____ different types of exam questions which may be used by college instructors.

18. If a true/false question says " _____ never occurs", and you don't know, you should answer:.
    _____ True   _____ False

19. In looking for organization patterns for thinking, reading, and writing, a person should know that one usual pattern is comparison- _____ .

20. Both reading and writing organization require that the details about a topic should be related to the
    a. title
    b. main idea
    c. author's opinion
    d. concluding statement.

ANSWER KEY:

1. (4) 2. (2) 3. (9) 4. (250) 5. (3) 6. (Review) 7. (80) 8. (b) 9. (a) 10. (50) 11. (5) 12. (d) 13. (Keywords) 14. (True) 15. (Do or Watch) 16. (True) 17. (6) 18. (False) 19. (Contrast) 20. (b)

Lesson 1: WHAT AM I DOING HERE ANYWAY?

Notes

Student Questionnaire on Motivation for College

TO THE STUDENT: Two things which can help you become a successful college student are a clear knowledge of why you are attending school at this moment, and an understanding of how you learn best. This lesson will guide you in acquiring this information.

Name _____ College Major _____

Reason for that Choice of Major _____

Ten years from now, how do you expect to be earning a living? _____
_____
_____

How does your choice of major relate to that job expectation? _____
_____
_____

   (If you don't know the answer to the above questions, simply write down two or three employment situations which seem interesting to you. Then list majors which are related to those jobs.)

   List the courses you will be taking this semester. Why are you enrolled in each one? How do you think each course relates to your future plans for employment or enrollment in graduate school?

© 1988 by Cambridge Stratford, LTD.

Lesson 1: WHAT AM I DOING HERE ANYWAY?

Notes

Which course do you expect to be the easiest for you? _____

Which will be the most difficult? _____

Estimate your quality (or grade) point average for this semester: _____

Course	Estimated Grade	Credit Hours	Quality Points

Total Quality Points _____

Divided by : Total Credit Hours _____

Equals : Quality Point Average _____

Notes

Learning Styles Preference Inventory

Directions: The letters on the right of this page stand for:

R – You would like to READ material on the subject: manuals, pamphlets, newspapers, textbooks, etc.
L – You would like to have someone tell you about something so you learn by LISTENING. (You may take notes.)
D – You would rather try to DO this yourself by acting it out, or making something, etc.;
W – You would like to WATCH a movie or some slides about the topic.

Each of the numbered statements refers to something you are going to learn and on which you will be <u>tested</u>. Write the number four (4) under the letter that best indicates how you would want to learn the material, lesson, etc. Then put a three (3) under the next best, a two (2) under the next, and a one (1) under the letter of the way in which you would least want to have to learn the material or lesson.

	R	L	D	W
1. How an African tribe plants its crops				
2. Keep the accounts for a small hardware store				
3. Choose costumes for a medieval play				
4. How to measure the pollution level in a body of water				
5. Why spark plugs wear out in engines				
6. Determining the amount of carpet needed for 3 rooms				
7. Writing a description of a club activity				
8. Make travel arrangements for your boss				
9. Why Henry VIII executed Ann Boleyn				
10. Determine the guilty party in a crime				
11. Find the result of mixing two chemicals				
12. Recite the major bones in the human body				
13. Decorate your first apartment				
14. How to play tennis				
15. Recite Hamlet's "To Be or Not to Be" Soliloquy				
Now add the columns. Totals:				

© 1988 by Cambridge Stratford, LTD.

Lesson 1: WHAT AM I DOING HERE ANYWAY?

Notes

Personal Assessment Form

Name _____

   My score on the study skills pre-test is _____. According to my inventory, my strongest learning mode is _____, and my weakest area is _____. For my current schedule of classes, my best approach for each class would be:

_____   _____
            _____
_____   _____
            _____
_____   _____
            _____
_____   _____
            _____
_____   _____
            _____

To overcome my weakness in learning in the _____ mode, I will attempt to

1. _____
   _____
2. _____
   _____
3. _____
   _____

For each of these, I will plan to do the following in the <u>next</u> week:

1. _____
   _____
2. _____
   _____
3. _____
   _____

© 1988 by Cambridge Stratford, LTD.

Notes:

References

Pauk, Walter. How to Study In College, Second Edition. Boston, Mass.: Houghton Mifflin Co., 1974, pp. 1-99.

McWhorter, Kathleen. College Reading and Study Skills, Third Edition. Boston, Mass.: Little, Brown and Company, 1986, pp. 12-25.

Shepherd, James. The Houghton Mifflin Reading, Study and Vocabulary Program. Boston, Mass.: Houghton Mifflin Co., 1981, pp. 1-20.

Time Management

Lesson 2:
TIME FLIES WHEN YOU ARE HAVING FUN!

Objective:

1. The student will recognize the importance of efficient use of time.

2. The student should be able to plan the amount of time he/she should spend in studying each week.

3. The student will produce a weekly schedule to be used as a guide for one semester.

4. The student should be able to relate the planning for one semester to the need for a weekly schedule for use of study time.

Lesson 2: TIME FLIES WHEN YOU ARE HAVING FUN!

Notes:

College can and should be an enjoyable time of life, but a good student must balance college classroom activities, outside activities which are also learning experiences, and the activities which are necessary to just live a life. In addition, we all want to have some time to relax and just have FUN! Time slips away from us very easily. To help you, the student, make the most of your time, and to ensure a sufficient amount of time is spent in study, it is useful to analyze personal use of time, learn the best times and the amount of time needed to study, and then PLAN an appropriate schedule.

To provide a picture of how your time is usually spent, work with your instructor to fill in the weekly schedule labeled No. 1 on page 11. Be as complete and as accurate as you can. Use short labels to identify what you usually do in particular hours, such as: TV; FOOD; SHOWER; TRAVEL; CLASS; PARTY; WORK; LAUNDRY; TALK (to friends or dormmates); etc.

When you have labeled blocks of time for all the activities mentioned by your instructor, count the remaining hours. DON'T COUNT THE HOURS YOU WOULD NORMALLY BE SLEEPING! (Remember, this is a time for accuracy and honesty!)

Lesson 2: TIME FLIES WHEN YOU ARE HAVING FUN!

WEEKLY PLANNER/RECORDER

	MONDAY	TUESDAY	WEDNESDAY	THURSDAY	FRIDAY	SATURDAY	SUNDAY
6:00 / 6:30							
7:00 / 7:30							
8:00 / 8:30							
9:00 / 9:30							
10:00 / 10:30							
11:00 / 11:30							
12:00 / 12:30							
1:00 / 1:30							
2:00 / 2:30							
3:00 / 3:30							
4:00 / 4:30							
5:00 / 5:30							
6:00 / 6:30							
7:00 / 7:30							
8:00 / 8:30							
9:00 / 9:30							
10:00 / 10:30							
11:00 / 11:30							
12:00 / 12:30							

The Flaw in Paganism

Drink and dance and laugh and lie,
Love, the reeling midnight through,
For tomorrow we shall die!
(But, alas, we never do.)

-Dorothy Parker

© 1988 by Cambridge Stratford, LTD.

From The Portable Dorothy Parker, Copyright 1931, renewed © 1956 by Dorothy Parker. Reprinted by permission of Viking Penguin Inc.

Notes

The Moment of Truth

Fill in the blank: I now have about _____ hours during the week when I do not already have something filled in.

I am currently in classes which meet _____ hours each week. If I multiply that number by two (2), the result is _____ hours which I should probably use as a rule-of-thumb for the number of hours I should study each week.

Check the answer which best fits your schedule:

1. _____ I have enough hours left in my schedule so that I can fit in the number of hours I should spend studying.

2. _____ I have a schedule which is too busy. I need to make some adjustments as I plan my study schedule for this semester.

If you checked number 2, what is the difference between the number of hours you should probably spend studying, according to the two-to-one hour rule, and the number of hours you currently have available for study? _____

Think about your schedule. Look at it. Where can you find these hours? What has to be removed from your current weekly schedule? Are you sleeping too much? Are you working too many hours at your job? Do you watch too much TV? Are you spending too much time talking to friends or partying? What can you change to find the hours you need?

List two things you could do to change your schedule and get more time for your first priority – study:

1. _____
_____
_____
_____

2. _____
_____
_____
_____

Lesson 2: TIME FLIES WHEN YOU ARE HAVING FUN!

WEEKLY PLANNER/RECORDER

	MONDAY	TUESDAY	WEDNESDAY	THURSDAY	FRIDAY	SATURDAY	SUNDAY
6:00 6:30							
7:00 7:30							
8:00 8:30							
9:00 9:30							
10:00 10:30							
11:00 11:30							
12:00 12:30							
1:00 1:30							
2:00 2:30							
3:00 3:30							
4:00 4:30							
5:00 5:30							
6:00 6:30							
7:00 7:30							
8:00 8:30							
9:00 9:30							
10:00 10:30							
11:00 11:30							
12:00 12:30							

© 1988 by Cambridge Stratford, LTD.

Lesson 2: TIME FLIES WHEN YOU ARE HAVING FUN!

MONTHLY PLANNER/RECORDER

Month _____

SUNDAY	MONDAY	TUESDAY	WEDNESDAY	THURSDAY	FRIDAY	SATURDAY

© 1988 by Cambridge Stratford, LTD.

Lesson 2: TIME FLIES WHEN YOU ARE HAVING FUN!

MONTHLY PLANNER/RECORDER

Month _____

SUNDAY	MONDAY	TUESDAY	WEDNESDAY	THURSDAY	FRIDAY	SATURDAY

© 1988 by Cambridge Stratford, LTD.

Lesson 2: TIME FLIES WHEN YOU ARE HAVING FUN!

MONTHLY PLANNER/RECORDER

Month _____

SUNDAY	MONDAY	TUESDAY	WEDNESDAY	THURSDAY	FRIDAY	SATURDAY

© 1988 by Cambridge Stratford, LTD.

Lesson 2: TIME FLIES WHEN YOU ARE HAVING FUN!

MONTHLY PLANNER/RECORDER

Month _____

SUNDAY	MONDAY	TUESDAY	WEDNESDAY	THURSDAY	FRIDAY	SATURDAY

© 1988 by Cambridge Stratford, LTD.

MONTHLY PLANNER/RECORDER

Month _____

SUNDAY	MONDAY	TUESDAY	WEDNESDAY	THURSDAY	FRIDAY	SATURDAY

© 1988 by Cambridge Stratford, LTD.

Lesson 2: TIME FLIES WHEN YOU ARE HAVING FUN!

WEEKLY PLANNER/RECORDER

	MONDAY	TUESDAY	WEDNESDAY	THURSDAY	FRIDAY	SATURDAY	SUNDAY
6:00 / 6:30							
7:00 / 7:30							
8:00 / 8:30							
9:00 / 9:30							
10:00 / 10:30							
11:00 / 11:30							
12:00 / 12:30							
1:00 / 1:30							
2:00 / 2:30							
3:00 / 3:30							
4:00 / 4:30							
5:00 / 5:30							
6:00 / 6:30							
7:00 / 7:30							
8:00 / 8:30							
9:00 / 9:30							
10:00 / 10:30							
11:00 / 11:30							
12:00 / 12:30							

© 1988 by Cambridge Stratford, LTD.

Notes:

References

Cohen, King, Knudsvig, et al. Quest: Academic Skills Program. New York, New York: Harcourt Brace Jovanovich Inc., 1973, pp. 249-293.

McWhorter, Kathleen T. College Reading and Study Skills. Boston, Mass.: Little, Brown and Company, 1986, pp. 12-25.

Pauk, Walter. How to Study in College. Boston, Mass.: Houghton Mifflin Co., 1974, pp. 18-32.

Shepherd, James. RSVP The Houghton Mifflin Reading, Study and Vocabulary Program. Boston, Mass.: Houghton Mifflin Co., 1981, pp. 23-46.

Woods, Nancy V. College Reading and Study Skills. New York, New York: Holt, Reinhart and Winston, pp. 13-22.

Critical Thinking/Problem Solving

Lesson 3
THINKING CAPS IN PLACE NOW: LET'S TRY IT!

Objectives

1. The student will demonstrate a knowledge of the differences among literal, inferential, critical and analytical thinking.

2. The student should be able to demonstrate the ability to use different thinking skills for different tasks as he/she studies.

3. Given a problem, the student should be able to list the steps which must be taken to solve the problem.

4. The student will be able to give an example of convergent thinking and an example of divergent thinking and explain the difference.

Notes

Copyright 1985, U.S. News & World Report. Reprinted from Issue of November 25, 1985.

LOVE OF LEARNING STILL HAS A PLACE IN COLLEGE LIFE

BY William Bennett, U.S. Secretary of Education, in U.S. News & World Report

At college as a freshman some time ago, I had definite ideas about how I wanted to use my four years of higher education. I wanted to major in English because I wanted to become sophisticated. I wanted to become sophisticated because I wanted to land a good job and make big money.

But because of my college's course requirements, I found myself in an introductory philosophy class, confronted by Plato's "Republic" and a remarkable professor who knew how to make the text come alive. It seemed to me and many of my fellow classmates as if we had come face to face with a reincarnation of Socrates himself. Before we knew it, we were ensnared by the power of a 2,000-year-old dialogue.

In our posture of youthful cynicism and arrogance, we at first resisted the idea that the question of justice should really occupy our time. But something happened to us that semester as we fought our way through the "Republic," arguing about notions of right and wrong. Along the way, our insides were shaken up a little bit.

Without quite knowing it, we had committed ourselves to the serious enterprise of raising and wrestling with questions. And once caught up in that enterprise, there was no turning back. We had met up with a great text and a great teacher; they had taken us, and we were theirs.

Every student is entitled to that kind of experience at college. And if I could make one request of future undergraduates, it would be that they open the door to that possibility. College should shake you up a little, get you breathing, quicken your senses and animate a conscious examination of life's enduring questions. Know thyself, Socrates said. Higher education worthy of the name aspires to nothing less than the wisdom of that dictum.

Those are lofty ambitions. What do they mean in the context of four years of campus life? A college is many things. It is a collection of dormitories, libraries, social clubs, incorrigibly terrible cafeterias. But above all, it is a faculty. It used to be said, when this country was much younger, that a log lying on the side of the road with a student sitting on one end and a professor on the other was a university.

That essence has not changed. It is the relationship between teachers and their students that gives a campus its own special genius. "Like a contagious disease, almost," William James wrote, "spiritual life passes from man to man by contact." Above all, a student should

Lesson 3: THINKING CAPS IN PLACE NOW: LET'S TRY IT!

Notes

look for – and expect to find – professors who can bring to life the subject at hand.

What else should students find at college? They should discover great works that tell us how men and women of our own and other civilizations have grappled with life's relentless questions: What should be loved? What deserves to be defended? What is noble and what is base? As Montaigne wrote, a student should have the chance to learn "what valor, temperance, and justice are; and the difference between ambition and greed, loyalty and servitude, liberty and license; and the marks of true and solid contentment."

This means, first of all, that students should find wide exposure to all the major disciplines – history, science, literature, mathematics and foreign language. And it means that they should be introduced to the best that has been thought and written in every discipline.

College is, for many, a once-in-a-lifetime chance to discover our civilization's greatest achievements and lasting visions. There are many great books, discoveries and deeds that record those achievements in unequaled fashion. There are many more that do not. A good college will sort the great texts and important ideas from the run-of-the-mill and offer the best to its students. And that offering will be the institution's vision of a truly educated person.

All students have different notions about where they want a college degree to take them. For some, it is law school or journalism. For others, it's public service. That's fine. College should be a road to your ambitions. But every student should take the time to tread the ground outside his or her major, and to spend some time in the company of the great travelers who have come before.

Why? Put simply, because they can help you lead a better and perhaps happier life. If we give time to studying how men and women of the past have dealt with life's enduring problems, then we will be better prepared when those same problems come our way. We may be a little less surprised to find treachery at work in the world about us, a little less startled by unselfish devotion, a little readier to believe in the capacity of the human mind.

And what does that do for a future career? As Hamlet said, "readiness is all." In the end, the problems we face during the course of a career are the same kinds that we face in the general course of life. If you want to be a corporate executive, how can you learn about not missing the right opportunities? One way is to read "Hamlet." Do you want to learn about the dangers of overweening ambition? Read "Macbeth." Want to know the pitfalls of playing around on the job? Read "Anthony and Cleopatra." The importance of fulfilling the responsibilities entrusted to leadership? Read "King Lear."

Even in the modern world, it is still that peculiar mix of literature,

Notes

> science, history, math, philosophy and language that can help mature minds come to grips with the age-old issues, the problems that transverse every plane of life. Students who bring to college the willingness to seek out those issues, to enliven the spirit and broaden the mind, will be more likely to profit in any endeavor.

Lesson 3: THINKING CAPS IN PLACE NOW: LET'S TRY IT!

Notes

Comprehension Questions for William Bennett's Article

(?) 1. The book Dr. Bennett read in philosophy was by
   a. Socrates
   b. Plato
   c. Aeschylus
   d. Aristotle

(+) 2. The <u>Republic</u> was originally part of a school curriculum
   a. before the birth of Jesus Christ
   b. during the reign of Queen Elizabeth I
   c. in Germany in the 13th century
   d. during the 1800s in Greece

(!) 3. At least one course we can be sure Dr. Bennett would recommend for all undergraduates is
   a. French
   b. Shakespeare
   c. Anthropology
   d. Chemistry

(*) 4. For his own children, Dr. Bennett would probably favor
   a. a bachelor's degree in business
   b. a bachelor's degree in liberal arts
   c. an associate's degree in physical therapy
   d. an associate's degree in nursing

(+) 5. According to Bennett, a college should provide
   a. a liberal education
   b. the administration
   c. the faculty
   d. all of the above

(?) 6. Dr. Bennett said the most important thing on a college campus is
   a. the cafeteria
   b. the administration
   c. the faculty
   c. the library

(*) 7. As Secretary of Education, Mr. Bennett, we assume, is most interested in
   a. the publication of new textbooks
   b. building new schools
   c. faculty development
   d. financing schools and colleges

© 1988 by Cambridge Stratford, LTD.

Notes

(+) 8. The educational goal of an undergraduate should be
    a. to prepare for a career
    b. to learn to think
    c. to gain exposure to previous civilizations
    d. all of the above

(!) 9. An outstanding college professor, according to the author, should be first and foremost
    a. a brilliant researcher
    b. a well-published author
    c. a stimulating teacher
    d. an outstanding speaker

(?) 10. From this article, we know
    a. Bennett attended a four-year college
    b. Bennett attended a technical college
    c. Bennett attended a community college
    d. Bennett attended a church-related college

Lesson 3: THINKING CAPS IN PLACE NOW: LET'S TRY IT!

Notes

Answer key to comprehension questions on article by William Bennett

(?) 1. B   (+) 5. D
(+) 2. A   (*) 4. B
(!) 3. B   (!) 9. C
(*) 7. C   (?) 10. A
(?) 6. C
(+) 8. D

Key to types of questions

(?) - literal

(+) - inferential

(!) - critical

(*) - analytical

Notes

Problem 1 Recipe

Suppose you have to do six math problems for homework. You already know that each one will take you about ten minutes. It is now three o'clock in the afternoon. Math class is at ten o'clock tomorrow morning. You have English class at nine o'clock tomorrow.

Tonight there is a basketball game at 7:30, and you have planned a date for the game and for pizza afterwards.

Your advisor wants to see you at four o'clock today. The cafeteria is near your advisor's office. It is open for dinner from 4:30 to 6:30.

You need about thirty minutes for a shower, etc. before the game. You usually get up about eight o'clock in the morning.

When will you do your homework for math class? How will you decide? What is your 'recipe' for successful solving of this problem?

_____
_____
_____
_____
_____
_____
_____
_____
_____
_____
_____
_____
_____
_____
_____
_____
_____
_____
_____

Lesson 3: THINKING CAPS IN PLACE NOW: LET'S TRY IT!

Notes

Problem 2 Detective

An Internal Revenue Service employee was sorting through a number of tax returns which were on his desk. He entered some taxpayer information and a social security number for James Clinton in the computer. The computer printed the following information:

1976 Tax paid on $40,032 taxable income
1977 Tax paid on $43,289 taxable income
1978 Tax paid on $45,679 taxable income
1979 Tax paid on $47,232 taxable income
1980 Tax paid on $53,257 taxable income
1981 Tax paid on $13,247 taxable income
1982 Tax paid on $14,231 taxable income
1983 Tax paid on $13,978 taxable income

List three possible reasons for this reduced income.

_____

_____

_____

What questions would you ask, if you were the agent, to decide whether or not this account should be called in for an audit?

_____

_____

_____

_____

_____

_____

_____

_____

_____

_____

_____

_____

_____

Notes

Problem 3 Brainstorm

You have received permission to move off campus. Your parents are only willing to contribute the same amount of money, however, as they would have had to pay if you remained in the dormitory. Your current room and board costs at your college are $3000 per year. You own no furniture. The apartment which you want to rent is unfurnished, and costs $500 per month plus utilities. It has three bedrooms. You currently live in a dorm room which you share with one other person. You are a junior in college, and you have a work-study job which pays you $3.50 per hour. You currently work twenty hours each week when school is in session. You are a "B" student. You have a savings account which has a current balance of $600. You hope to go to law school when you graduate.

What is the information you must consider? What other things must you consider in making the decision? If you do move into the apartment, what must you do to be certain this will work out for you?

List five difficulties you must consider in making this decision.

_____
_____
_____
_____
_____

What are some of the possible solutions you might consider?

_____
_____
_____

Which of these solutions is the best, in your opinion, and WHY?

_____
_____
_____
_____
_____
_____
_____

Lesson 3: THINKING CAPS IN PLACE NOW: LET'S TRY IT!

Notes

Problem Solving
SUMMARY AND CONCLUSIONS

Problem 1:
_____
_____
_____
_____
_____
_____
_____
_____

Problem 2:
_____
_____
_____
_____
_____
_____
_____
_____

Problem 3:
_____
_____
_____
_____
_____
_____
_____
_____

Notes

References

Grinols, Anne Bradstreet. <u>Critical Thinking: Reading Across the Curriculum</u>. Cornell, New York: Cornell University Press, 1984.

Harris, Theodore L. and Eric J. Cooper. <u>Reading, Thinking, and Concept Development</u>. New York, New York: College Entrance Examination Board, 1985.

Miles, Curtis and Jane Rauton. <u>Thinking Tools: Academic, Personal, and Career Applications</u>. Clearwater, Florida: H & H Publishing Co., 1985.

Staton, Thomas F. and Emma D. Staton. <u>How to Study</u>, Sixth Edition. Nashville, Tenn.: How To Study, 1977, pp. 30-59.

Whimbey, Arthur. <u>Analytical Reading and Reasoning</u>. Stanford, Conn.: Innovative Sciences, Inc., 1983, pp. 123-158.

Whimbey, Arthur and Linda Whimbey. <u>Intelligence Can Be Taught</u>, Special Edition. Stanford, Conn.: Innovative Sciences, Inc., 1985.

Memorization

**Lesson 4:
ELEPHANTS NEVER FORGET: HOW ABOUT YOU?**

Objectives:

1. The student should be able to distinguish between short- and long-term memory.

2. The student will be able to define the concepts of motivation, selectivity, clarification, association and review in memorizing and studying material.

3. The student will be able to give an example of a subject which could be studied which would utilize the magic number seven method of memory.

4. The student will be able to define and give at least two examples of mnemonic devices and relate their use to college study.

© 1988 by Cambridge Stratford, LTD.

Notes:

Rate of Forgetting (with no review)

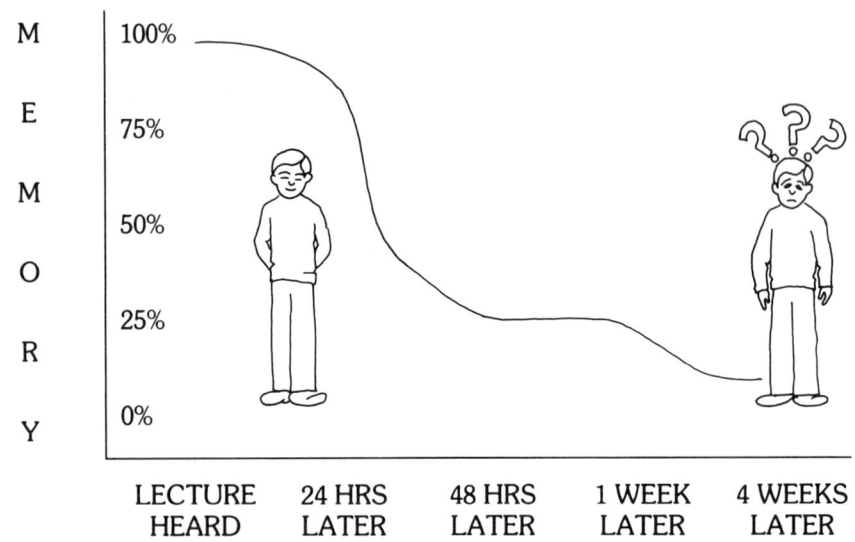

Rate of Forgetting (with 10 minutes review)

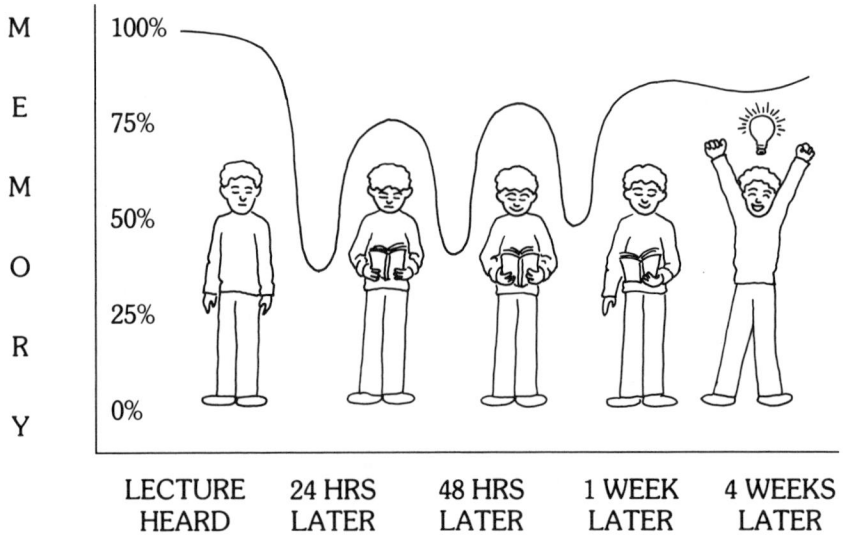

Lesson 4: ELEPHANTS NEVER FORGET: HOW ABOUT YOU?

Notes:

MAGIC NUMBER SEVEN

Classmates' Notes	Soap Names
1. _____	1. _____
2. _____	2. _____
3. _____	3. _____
4. _____	4. _____
5. _____	5. _____
6. _____	6. _____
7. _____	7. _____
8. _____	8. _____
9. _____	9. _____

ASSOCIATION

1. _____	1. _____
2. _____	2. _____
3. _____	3. _____
4. _____	4. _____
5. _____	5. _____
6. _____	6. _____
7. _____	7. _____
8. _____	8. _____
9. _____	9. _____
10. _____	10. _____

© 1988 by Cambridge Stratford, LTD.

Notes:

Five Essentials For Memorization

M – MOTIVATION
_____
_____
_____
_____

S – SELECTION
_____
_____
_____
_____

C – CLARIFICATION
_____
_____
_____
_____

A – ASSOCIATION
_____
_____
_____
_____

R – REVIEW
_____
_____
_____
_____

Lesson 4: ELEPHANTS NEVER FORGET: HOW ABOUT YOU? 37

NOTES:

Mnemonic Devices

Mnemonic Device I

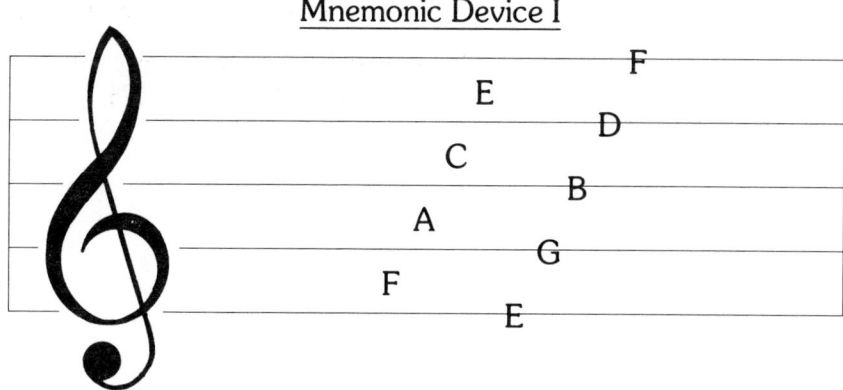

SPACES: F A C E = FACE
LINES: E G B D F = Every Good Boy Deserves Fun

Mnemonic Device II
Thirty days hath September

_____
_____
_____
_____
_____
_____

Other Mnemonics

_____
_____
_____
_____
_____
_____
_____

© 1988 by Cambridge Stratford, LTD.

Notes

References

McWhorter, Kathleen. <u>College Reading and Study Skills</u>. Boston, Mass.: Little, Brown and Company, 1986, pp. 26-38.

Pauk, Walter. <u>Essential Skills</u>, Book 16. Providence, Rhode Island: Jamestown Publishers, 1976.

Speed Reading

**Lesson 5:
READING RATES FOR COLLEGE: LIFE IN THE FAST LANE**

Objectives:

1. The student will recognize at least three different reading rates to be used for three different purposes in college reading tasks.

2. The student should be able to determine his/her own current reading rate.

3. The student will establish a goal and a personal plan to double his/her reading rate within a four week period.

Notes:

Reprinted with permission from Psychology Today Magazine, Copyright 1986 (APA)

Do Seat Belts Kill?

By Kevin Krajick

The British Parliament's recent decision to extend its country's three-year-old mandatory seat belt law has put the spotlight on a controversial theory: that vehicle-safety devices may actually do harm, because drivers compensate for increased protection by driving faster and more carelessly.

Legislators hotly debated the theory, often referred to as "risk compensation," with seat belt proponents labeling it "eccentric," "absurd" and "bogus." Still, the dispute continues among safety experts both in Britain and the United States, where 17 states and the District of Columbia have recently passed seat-belt laws.

One of the main proponents of risk compensation is John Adams, a geographer at University College in London. Adams cites official statistics showing that although driver deaths declined after the law's original passage in 1983, deaths among bicyclists, pedestrians, and back-seat passengers (who usually don't wear belts) climbed, wiping out much of the savings in drivers' lives.

"Protecting car occupants from the consequences of bad driving encourages bad driving," Adams says. He contends that the belted-in drivers end up bumping off others because they feel safer themselves.

Evidence that drivers adjust their behavior according to the features of their cars goes back well before modern safety features. In 1938, researchers concluded that with newly efficient braking systems in American cars, drivers quickly learned that they could afford to make shorter stops, and proceeded to do so consistently. A decade ago, Swedish psychologist Kare Rumar and colleagues found that drivers who had cars equipped with studded snow tires took curves faster than those who did not.

In case of seat belts, a study commissioned by the British Department of Transport concluded that despite the apparent "mystery" of increased nondriver deaths, there was still a net savings of 200 lives a year.

This sort of calculation runs counter to the theories of Gerald Wilde, a professor of psychology at Queen's University in Kingston, Ontario. Over time, according to Wilde, people will always adjust their behavior in such a way as to offset the overall effects of any safety improvement. He calls this "risk homeostasis." His detractors call it "Wilde's Theory of the Conservation of Misery."

Wilde asserts that every society has a built-in target level of danger people are willing to accept in exchange for the benefits they believe they accrue, such as getting to work on time or deriving pleasure from driving. This target level functions as a kind of danger thermostat: Devices that make drivers safer, he argues, provoke a collective increase in risky behavior.

Lesson 5: READING RATES FOR COLLEGE: LIFE IN THE FAST LANE

Notes:

In one of the few lab studies to test the notion of risk compensation, Wilde asked college undergraduates to switch off the light that appeared at random intervals on a computer screen. He told them that the closer they came to switching the light off 800-milliseconds after it appeared, the more money they would make, but if they took longer than 800 milliseconds, they would lose part of their pay. In fact, the students were not always penalized for exceeding the 800-millisecond limit. At various intervals the odds that the computer would "catch" and penalize those who pushed their luck too far changes.

Wilde found that though the students were not told of the fluctuating risks they faced, they nevertheless adjusted their reponses when the threat changed. On average, when the probability that the computer would penalize them was relatively high, students acted more conservatively, taking less time to switch off the light than when the threat was relatively low. Based on these results and those of other studies, Wilde contends that people adjust their behavior even in response to changes in the environment that are not readily apparent – a controversial assertion even among many of those who support a theory of at least partial risk compensation.

Only devices that provide direct feedback about vehicle performance, such as brakes and high-friction tires, can bring about a compensating reaction, argues Brian O'Neill, president of the Insurance Institute for Highway Safety, a research organization sponsored by the insurance industry. He discounts such features as energy-absorbing steering columns and penetration-resistant windshields – both of which have become standard equipment in recent years. "Not one person in a hundred knows those things exist. How can they react?" He asks.

He also deletes seat belts from the list, discounting the idea that "any normal person goes through a thought process that says: 'Now I'm safer, so I can drive faster.' " Studies conducted by the institute in 1982 and 1983, before and after Britain and Newfoundland put their seat-belt laws into effect, found no significant changes in speed or other safety indicators, such as following distance between cars.

Leonard Evans, a senior staff research scientist for General Motors, has done perhaps the most thorough research of studies on risk compensation. In a paper published last October, Evans, a physicist, concludes that drivers' reaction to safety – or the lack of it – can go in any number of directions.

In his own research, Evans found that although occupants of small cars are more likely to be killed if they have a crash, drivers of such cars actually have 28 percent fewer accidents – a fact that he attributes,

Notes:

in part, to increased caution due to the increased danger. (Unfortunately, small-car drivers don't seem to compensate enough, for even though involved in fewer accidents overall, they still have a higher chance of getting killed.)

On the other hand, Evans cites studies done in Detroit and Ontario suggesting that many of those who wear seat belts – and who presumably are better protected from the effects of crashes – also drive more safely, traveling more slowly and allowing more headway between vehicles than do those who do not buckle up. "The buckling of the seat belt may be an opportune reminder that crashes do, in fact, occur, and may induce more cautious driving," Evans suggests.

But he also agrees with the classic risk compensation argument in some cases, pointing out that radar systems do not seem to have reduced accidents in foggy weather. He also cites studies from Ireland and Canada indicating that seat belt laws there have fallen short of producing the safety benefit that engineers had predicted.

Scientists on different sides of the question do appear to agree on one thing: the need for road and vehicle designers to consider more often the possible human responses to engineering advances. "Modern inventions don't exist in a vacuum," Adams says. "People choose to be as safe as they want to be."

Whether this is true or not, 90 percent of British drivers choose to obey the seat-belt law, unlike their counterparts in the United States, of whom as many as half violate such statutes.

Does Adams buckle up when he gets behind the wheel? "If I were in America, I'd plead the Fifth on that," he replies.

Lesson 5: READING RATES FOR COLLEGE: LIFE IN THE FAST LANE

Notes:

Comprehension Questions For "Do Seat Belts Kill?"

1. The main idea of this article concerns
   - a. seat belts
   - b. auto deaths
   - c. risk compensation
   - d. highway safety

2. Drivers of small cars have fewer accidents than big cars by what percent?
   - a. fifty-two percent
   - b. twenty-eight percent
   - c. ten percent
   - d. highway safety

3. Studded tires encourage faster driving during the winter.

   True or False?

4. In Britain, 90% of the drivers use their seat belts. In the U.S., the experts estimate this drops to
   - a. seventy-five percent
   - b. fifty percent
   - c. twenty-five percent
   - d. forty-three percent

5. Professor Wilde calls the risk factor in driving
   - a. risk monitor
   - b. risk compensation
   - c. risk homeostasis
   - d. risk expectation

6. A millisecond is
   - a. 1/1000th of a second
   - b. 1/10th of a second
   - c. 1/100th of a second
   - d. 1/10,000 of a second

7. In 1983, driver deaths in Britain declined.

   True of False?

8. In the United States, there are mandatory seat belt laws in the District of Columbia and
   - a. ten states
   - b. fifty states
   - c. forty-eight states
   - d. seventeen states

9. Sometimes, car passengers are in danger BECAUSE the driver wears a seat belt.

   True or False?

10. The word <u>eccentric</u> means
    - a. quaint
    - b. beautiful
    - c. ordinary
    - d. worried

Lesson 5: READING RATES FOR COLLEGE: LIFE IN THE FAST LANE

Notes:

Reading Rates Chart	**1100 Work Article**
MINUTES	WORD RATE PER MINUTE
1:00	1100
1:30	733
1:40	660
1:50	600
2:00	550
2:10	508
2:20	471
2:30	440
2:40	413
2:50	388
3:00	367
3:10	347
3:20	330
3:30	314
3:40	300
3:50	287
4:00	275
4:10	264
4:20	254
4:30	244
4:40	236
4:50	228
5:00	220
5:10	213
5:20	206
5:30	200
5:40	194
5:50	189
6:00	183
6:10	178
6:20	174
6:30	169
6:40	165
6:50	161
7:00	157

© 1988 by Cambridge Stratford, LTD.

Lesson 5: READING RATES FOR COLLEGE: LIFE IN THE FAST LANE

Notes:

Column Reading Exercise

Human beings find it
Easier to read
For comprehension and speed
When articles are written
In a column.
Newspapers print
News in columns
So people can read
The paper quickly.
The average American reads
250 words per minute
After graduation
From high school;
That is about the rate
At which he speaks.
Yet it is possible to read
At a much faster rate
Because our brains can work
Faster than that.
With a few weeks of practice,
And intention to learn,
All of us could double
Our reading speed.

Time: _____

Rate: _____

Comprehension: _____

CAN YOU ANSWER THESE QUESTIONS?

1. The average WPM rate for American is _____.

2. Americans speak at about _____ words per minute.

3. In a few weeks, people could learn to read _____ as fast as they currently do.

4. To do this requires intention to learn and _____.

5. Columns are used most frequently by _____.

Lesson 5: READING RATES FOR COLLEGE: LIFE IN THE FAST LANE

For each correct answer, give yourself 20 points.

Notes:

Reprint from "Some Leaders Are Born Women" by Owen Findsen, <u>Gannett News Service</u>, March 23, 1986 © 1986.

Key Word Reading

MARILYN MACH VOS SAVANT is considered, by the <u>Guinness Book of Records</u>, the WORLD'S SMARTEST WOMAN. Her IQ SCORE is 230 on the Binet Test. The AVERAGE SCORE for that test is ONLY 100.

Interestingly, the word "SAVANT" means a LEARNED PERSON, a scholar. It comes from the FRENCH word "savoir" which means "to know." In 1985, the <u>OMNI IQ TEST QUIZ CONTEST</u>, a book, was published by McGraw-Hill. The AUTHOR is MS. VOS SAVANT.

MS. VOS SAVANT offers THREE RULES for becoming more intelligent. They are: (1) stop drawing conclusions; (2) stop answering questions unless you really know the correct answer; and (3) admit what you don't know and admit your errors.

Lesson 5: READING RATES FOR COLLEGE: LIFE IN THE FAST LANE

Notes:

Questions For Key Word Reading

1. What does savant mean?
   _____

2. What is the average score on the Binet?
   _____

3. What is Ms. Vos Savant's score on the Binet?
   _____

4. Ms. vos Savant says a person should remember _____ things if he wishes to raise his intelligence level.

5. When was her book published? _____.

Notes:

Copyright 1985 by Jay S. Albanese, Ph.D. University Press of America, Inc.

DEALING WITH DELINQUENCY

An Investigation of Juvenile Justice

Jay S. Albanese, Ph.D.

UNIVERSITY PRESS OF AMERICA

LANHAM • NEW YORK • LONDON

© 1988 by Cambridge Stratford, LTD.

Lesson 5: READING RATES FOR COLLEGE: LIFE IN THE FAST LANE

Notes:

A SYSTEM OF JUSTICE

Let us assume that you have the opportunity to form a new country on an uninhabited island. Before you know it, there are several thousand people on your island, and you are starting to get some serious complaints. You are hearing disputes over property rights, reports of thefts, quarreling, and even a few fist fights.

After a few months of this, the residents of your island community are becoming dissatisfied with your decisions in these cases and demand a democratic and impartial system for settling these disputes. In effect, you are being asked to set up a justice system.

As you attempt to do this, you face some fundamental questions that must be answered. What should the goal of the system be? Merely fairness? Deterrence of future misbehavior? Reformation of rule violators?

If you are going to set up a system of adjudication, you will also have to be specific about its jurisdiction. Over what types of acts will the justice system have authority? As a result, it will be necessary to codify behaviors that are subject to adjudication. Those actions that threaten the social order will probably be grouped in a criminal code.

The next question that arises is how broad or narrow do you wish to make the code? It is likely that crimes of assault (murder, rape, robbery) will be included, as will crimes of theft (burglary, larceny, motor vehicle theft). But will you include acts that involve voluntary participation by the victim and offender, such as prostitution, gambling, or drug use? Will you include status offenses such as runaways or truancy? These are difficult decisions that are ultimately left up to legislators in a democratic society who act on behalf of the community they represent.

Once the criminal code is established, however, it will not be self-enforcing. Who will make sure that all people in your country abide by the code of behavior? Once a society reaches a size where self-protection is no longer feasible, the legislature will establish an agency of law enforcement to apprehend law violators. But then, additional questions will arise. How much authority should

Notes:

you give the law enforcement agency? When may they encroach upon private property? When may they search a person? How do you best balance the enforcement of the code with the rights of individuals? These are questions that are still being answered in the United States today through court decisions and new legislation.

Let us assume that you manage to resolve these dilemmas. What happens when the law enforcement people catch a suspected code violator? Can the person be put in jail prior to a judgement against him? How positive must you be before you can treat a suspected law violator as an offender: reasonably sure, somewhat convinced, absolutely positive? If, through your adjudication process, you find a person guilty of the violation alleged, on what basis do you sanction him? Retribution? Incapacitation? Deterrence? Reformation?

As you can see, the establishment of a system of justice arises out of necessity in a country, simply because not all people will agree on accepted forms of conduct in a society. Once a system is established, however, the procedures for dealing with code violators must address issues of purpose, privacy, fairness, and justice--issues that do not always have easy answers.

A DIFFERENCE IN RESPONSIBILITY

Let us assume that, as time goes on, you feel that younger citizens in your country ought to be treated differently than older citizens in the justice process. That is, you believe that adults are (and should be) more responsible for their actions than juveniles and, therefore, should be treated differently. This is the conclusion that was reached in the United States when the first juvenile court was established in 1899.

As Table 1 indicates, the juvenile justice system uses different terminology than the adult system, illustrating the difference in philosophy. The juvenile justice system has more neutral terminology, whereas the adult system is an adversary system with formal accusations and convictions.

The establishment of the juvenile court corresponded with the rise of positivism which saw crimes as the product of internal or external influences, rather than the result of free-will.

Lesson 5: READING RATES FOR COLLEGE: LIFE IN THE FAST LANE

Notes:

Table 1. Adult & Juvenile Justice System Terminology.

Procedure	Juvenile	Adult
Act	Delinquency	Crime
Apprehension	Take into Custody Petition	Arrest Indictment
Pre-Adjudication	Detention Agree to finding Deny the petition	Jail Plead Guilty Plead not guilty
Adjudication	Adjudicatory Hearing Adjudicated Delinquent	Trial Convicted Criminal
Corrections	Disposition Hearing Disposition Commitment	Sentencing Sentence Incarceration

Logically, what is seen as the fundamental cause of human behavior will be reflected in the systems established to deal with it. If juvenile delinquency is seen as the result of environmental influences, for example, a justice process will attempt to correct the influences, or to correct the way the juvenile responds to these influences. On the other hand, if crime is seen as the product of one's free will, the only logical way to deal with it is through punishment to deter future misbehavior. In this way, people will guide their freely-willed actions accordingly. Unfortunately, prevailing views regarding the responsibility and treatment of juveniles have shifted over the years.

THREE MODELS OF JUVENILE JUSTICE

Currently, there is much disagreement over the proper goals of the juvenile justice system. This disagreement can be traced to the philosophical differences between the classical and positive schools of criminology. For example, it is often said that the United States must concentrate more fully on "law and order," which usually suggests the view that society needs to be protected from criminals. From another constituency, it is often said that we have to do our best to make law violators, especially juvenile delinquents, into "productive citizens." This usually

Notes:

indicates the view that criminals have problems that society should seek to correct. Still a third group claims that individual freedoms should be protected at all costs. Governments exist at the pleasure of the people, and the ability of the government to interfere in the lives of its citizens should be severely restricted. This focus on "individual protections" reflects the view that citizens must be adequately protected from the arbitrary exercise of governmental power.

It is probably true that everyone gives at least some credence to each of these three perspectives. Nevertheless, we usually see one view as being more important than the others. Depending upon what you see as the overriding goal of juvenile justice, this "philosophy" will be reflected in your view of a properly functioning juvenile justice system.

Table 2 represents how the juvenile justice system would work under each of the primary goals of law and order, productive citizens, and individual protections. The <u>crime control model</u> represents the law and order view. <u>According to this model</u>, the rights of the community are paramount with efficiency important to repress crime. Also, there would be a presumption of guilt for those reaching the adjudicatory stage because more weight would be placed on police decisions. Following the classical view, the punishment would fit the crime, assuming that all men are equal in their ability to choose among alternate courses of conduct.

The <u>rehabilitative model</u> places the needs of the <u>individual as a paramount</u> concern, and the justice system is based on a presumption of need. Following the positivistic view that delinquency results from internal or external influences, the juvenile would be treated according to the type of problem he or she manifested. Unlike the crime control model, the act itself would not be of great importance because it is only a symptom of some underlying problem that needs to be addressed.

The <u>due process model</u> is based on a presumption of innocence and places the rights of the individual as an overriding concern. in dealing with delinquency. Unlike the crime control model, accuracy and fairness are seen as being much more important than efficiency. The trial or adjudicatory hearing would be the most important part of the process because it is at this stage where the protection of

-43-

Lesson 5: READING RATES FOR COLLEGE: LIFE IN THE FAST LANE

Notes:

Table 2. Models of Juvenile Justice.

	LAW	POLICE	DETENTION	ADJUDICATION	DISPOSITION
CRIME CONTROL GOAL Increase efficiency in screening suspects, determining guilt, & dispositions to repress criminal behavior.	Legal definition of delinquency broad. Behavior seen as leading to delinquency should be adjudicated.	Increased power to search, arrest, and interrogate. Arrest decision would be considered correct for most part.	Would be extensively used to incapacitate juveniles so they could not commit other crimes while awaiting adjudication.	Relatively unimportant. Swift resolution of cases necessary to minimize delay. Assumption of efficient police work.	Punishment would fit crime rather than offender. Goal to reduce crime through incapacitation and deterrence.
REHABILITATIVE GOAL "Guilt" not relevant because juvs cannot be held fully responsible. Delinquency is a symptom of underlying problems to be addressed by juv. justice sys.	Legal definition of delinquency broad. Harmful behaviors may indicate underlying social or psychological problems.	Police would have juvenile specialists trained in psy and social diagnosis and treatment to identify problems early.	Would not be used very often, only in cases where juvenile needs protection or special care.	Guilt or innocence not very important. Focus on juv's psychological and social condition. Informal hearing designed to help juvenile.	Juvenile would be placed in once of a wide range of programs based on psychological or social needs (Not according to particular act committed)
DUE PROCESS GOAL Accuracy & fairness more important than efficiency. Gov't must be limited in ability to accuse citizens of crime & to deny one's civil liberties via adjudication	Legal definition of delinquency narrow. Vague or ambiguous definitions eliminated. Status offenses eliminated.	Police arrests, searches, and interrogations would be carefully reviewed to prevent abuses of power and of individual rights.	Not extensively used. Detention only employed with careful attention to individual rights. Hearing would be required.	Trial most important part of process to insure accuracy of facts and fairness in proceeding against defendant by the govt	Not so much concerned with content or rationale for penalty as with fairness in decisionmaking process. Unequal sentences not tolerated.

Notes:

individual rights and the accuracy of the allegations of misconduct can be most closely scrutinized.

These three models of alternative justice systems illustrate how one's philosophy of justice lies at the foundation of any justice syste . A society's assumptions regarding the causes of misconduct and the relationship between the individual and his government translate into the procedure by which those accused of crimes are treated. This distinction among the three models of justice will become increasingly significant in subsequent chapters when we will see that the rehabilitative model, based on positivism, formed the philosophy of juvenile court procedure from its inception until the 1960s. Evidence will be provide to show that a due process emphasis became apparent during the 1960s through the mid-1970s. Finally, recent events in juvenile justice will illustrate a contemporary trend toward the crime control model during the last 10 years.

REFERENCES

Faust, Frederic L. and Brantingham, Paul J. Models of Juvenile Justice: Introduction and Overview. In Juvenile Justice Philosophy. [Second Edition]. St Paul, Minn.: West Publishing, 1979.

Packer, Herbert L. The Limits of the Criminal Sanction. Stanford, Ca.: Stanford University Press, 1968.

Lesson 5: READING RATES FOR COLLEGE: LIFE IN THE FAST LANE

Notes:

Rapid Textbook Chapter Survey

Title of Chapter: _____

Are there graphic aids in the text (pictures, graphs, maps)? _____

Is there a summary at the end of the chapter? _____

What do you think this chapter will be about?
_____
_____

How many pages of reading are in the chapter? _____

Are you familiar with this material? _____

Approximately how long will it take you to read it? _____

_____
_____
_____
_____
_____
_____
_____
_____
_____
_____
_____
_____
_____
_____
_____
_____
_____

© 1988 by Cambridge Stratford, LTD.

Notes:

Reprinted with permission from <u>Psychology Today Magazine</u>. Copyright 1986 (APA)

How Much Sleep Is Enough?

Most newborn babies sleep 17 or 18 hours per day. By age 10, this has dropped to 9 to 10 hours, and it continues declining during adolescence. Two-thirds of adults sleep seven to eight hours per night, while one-fifth of adults sleep less than six hours and one-tenth sleep more than nine. During old age, sleep diminishes to an average of 6.5 hours a night. For the average adult, then, seven or eight hours a night is "normal." But is it necessary?

Some good sleepers worry that they regularly fall short of the Big Eight. They needn't. Psychologist Wilse Webb, at the University of Florida, psychiatrist Ernest Hartmann at Tufts University School of Medicine in Boston and others have found that those who naturally sleep less than six hours a night are happier, better adjusted and more active than longer sleepers. Such people, says the University of Arizona's Larry Beutler, may "have their whole nervous system wired quite efficiently. They may have more energy, make more social contacts and establish better social-support systems than more sluggish people.

Some people fear insomnia and its presumed effects so strongly that the fears aggravate their sleeplessness. But what's the real effect of a few lost hours? Several sleep-restriction studies have shown that one rotten night (with as little as two hours of sleep) doesn't really affect people's performance the next day, although they may feel more irritable, hostile, fatigued or unhappy.

William Dement and Mary Carskadon (then at Stanford) found in another study that when young adults get only five hours of sleep a night for a week, some become "pathologically sleepy" by the week's end. But the cumulative effects disappear after one good night's sleep.

Sleep deprivation can have devastating effects if it is total. Psychologist Allan Rechtschaffen of the University of Chicago produces profound, lethal, metabolic changes in rats totally deprived of sleep from less than a week to more than a month. But true sleep deprivation is very hard to arrange, since animals and humans sneak in "micro-sleeps." Long-suffering chronic insomniacs may say they "never catch a wink of sleep," but they're rarely totally sleep deprived, and usually get at least a few hours a night.

Lesson 5: READING RATES FOR COLLEGE: LIFE IN THE FAST LANE 57

Notes:

How Much Sleep Is Enough?

1. What percent of adults sleep more than nine hours a night?

    a. 10   b. 50   c. 66

2. A one night loss of sleep affects job performance.

    a. True   b. False

3. How many hours does a newborn usually sleep each day?

    a. 23   b. 10   c. 18

4. Total sleep deprivation can be lethal.

    a. True   b. False

5. Happy, adjusted, active adults usually sleep how many hours a night?

    a. less than 9   b. less than 7   c. less than 6

_____
_____
_____
_____
_____
_____
_____
_____
_____
_____
_____
_____
_____

Lesson 5: READING RATES FOR COLLEGE: LIFE IN THE FAST LANE

Notes:

Double Your Reading Rate In Just Four Weeks

An average reader can double his/her reading rate in just four weeks with steady practice and a strong intention to achieve. Select any novel with which to practice. Begin the daily process by "reading" just as quickly as you can for five minutes. This "reading" is not an exercise in comprehension. You will not be able to comprehend everything you look at; you are simply trying to move your eyes as quickly as you can over the words. DO NOT SKIP WORDS. KEEP YOUR EYES ON THE PAGE!

At the end of five minutes, count the number of words you have "read" and record that number in the proper column on your RATE RECORDING CHART. Divide by five (5) to get your average word per minute at this rapid rate.

Continue to read for the next fifteen minutes, but now read at your normal rate. At the end of the fifteen minutes, enter the number of words you read and again divide to get your rate for one minute.

DO THIS EACH DAY FOR FOUR WEEKS. YOUR EYES AND YOUR BRAIN WILL BE ACCUSTOMED TO THE FASTER RATE AND YOU WILL BEGIN TO COMPREHEND MORE EACH DAY. AT THE END OF FOUR WEEKS, YOU SHOULD HAVE DOUBLED YOUR READING RATE FOR THE READING OF NOVELS. AND, YOU WILL HAVE READ THAT NOVEL YOU "HAVE BEEN MEANING TO READ FOR THE LONGEST TIME"!

Lesson 5: READING RATES FOR COLLEGE: LIFE IN THE FAST LANE

Notes:

Double Your Reading Rate Four Week Chart

Day	NORMAL RATE		RAPID RATE		Gain
	5 Min.	1 Min.	5 Min.	1 Min.	
1					
2					
3					
4					
5					
6					
7					
8					
9					
10					
11					
12					
13					
14					
15					
16					
17					
18					
19					
20					
21					
22					
23					
24					
25					
26					
27					
28					

Beginning Rate _____ WPM

Ending Rate _____ WPM

Gain _____ WPM

© 1988 by Cambridge Stratford, LTD.

Notes:

Reprinted with permission of Saturday Review, from May/June 1985 issue.

Baseball Dreams

By Don Freeman

MEMORABLE QUOTES ABOUT BASEBALL

"Whoever wants to know the heart and mind of America had better learn baseball," wrote Jacques Barzun in a line he may regret having written, so platitudinous has it become in its retelling. As Hemingway was to the bullfight, many American writers have been to baseball, rhapsodizing over what is essentially a simple exercise whose every nuance is known instinctively to small boys before they have mastered fractions.

Listen to them: "One reason I have always loved baseball so much," wrote Thomas Wolfe, "is that it has been not merely 'the great national game,' but really a part of the whole weather of our lives, of the thing that is our own, of the whole fabric, the million memories of America."

"By and large," wrote David Halberstam, "it is the sport that a foreigner is least likely to take to. You have to grow up playing it, you have to accept the love of the bubble-gum card and believe that if the answer to the Mays-Snider-Mantle question is found, then the universe will be a simpler and ordered place."

And from Walt Whitman: "I see great things in baseball. It's our game – the American game."

OTHER QUOTES ABOUT BASEBALL

And it isn't just writers. Old generals also get poetically ecstatic. "When I was a boy growing up in Kansas," wrote Dwight D. Eisenhower, "a friend of mine and I went fishing and as we sat there in the warmth of a summer afternoon on a river bank we talked about what we wanted to do when we grew up. I told him I wanted to be a real major league baseball player, a genuine professional like Honus Wagner. My friend said that he'd like to be President of the United States. Neither of us got our wish."

The list of valentines to baseball is as long and endless as a Fourth of July doubleheader of old. But, of course, they lie. Or, put less harshly, they see the game in the russet glow of wistful and, alas, false remembrance.

Ask them, these idolaters, if they ever once struck out in the ninth inning with the winning run perched at third. Ask them if they ever threw wildly past first base, thus permitting the opposing nine to score the deciding run. Ask them if they ever dropped an easy fly ball to lose the old ball game.

Don't ask them. Ask me. I have committed all of the above. And therein lies the true soul, the Charlie Brown soul, the elusive mystique

Lesson 5: READING RATES FOR COLLEGE: LIFE IN THE FAST LANE

Notes:

of the game.

Baseball may seem to be a masculine sport of plain talk – a Harry Truman kind of game – but in reality it is a capriciously feminine inspirer of futile fantasies. Baseball is a pretty girl who declined our invitation to go to the movies on Saturday night because she said she had to wash her hair. And then we asked her to go to the prom six weeks hence, and she said she had plans on the very night to wash her hair again. And we believed her. And we loved her still. It is defined as the national pastime, but what baseball really is, beneath the benign facade, is a metaphor for the national rebuff.

Growing up in Chicago, I was slightly cuckoo about baseball, but baseball responded to my ardor with disdain. Playing this game that consumed my thoughts while yielding no solace, I was loud but mediocre. I "talked it up." But I was a weak stick and my fielding was uncertain. I was also slow afoot – as the old line went, there was larceny in my heart but my feet were honest. And yet I nourished my secret fantasy, which was to play shortstop for the hometown Cubs. A small, snickering voice whispered to me: "Listen, kid, face it – you ain't even a regular on your high school team so how could you ever be a big league shortstop?" I heard the small voice and I told it to get lost.

But the fantasy persisted, a white whale to my Ahab. And it lingers on into middle age, for in my dreams at night I see myself roaming stylishly on the greensward and I move with the easy fluidity and grace of a Marty Marion, who played shortstop for the St. Louis Cardinals and was tall and rangy, both of which I am not except in my dreams. In those dreams my uniform is interchangeable. I play for the Cubs and Cards and Giants and Pirates, but never the Yankees or White Sox. I am strictly a National League dreamer. I will see myself playing – no, starring! – for the Cubs and we are in Chicago's Wrigley Field. I am Billy Jurges at short and I handle a hard-hit grounder with ease, flipping the ball with a certain insouciance to Billy Herman at second and he in turn throws it to Phil Cavaretta for the double play. It is lovely.

My first memory of listening to the radio was pressing an ear to broadcasts of major league baseball. How vivid those broadcasts were! How much more vivid they were than the picture on a television screen would be in later years. The ballparks described by announcers on the radio of my boyhood seemed a magic Oz.

I reveled in the nicknames of baseball – Lon Warneke was the "Arkansas Hummingbird," Guy Bush was the "Mississippi Mudcat," and they pitched for my beloved Cubs. They had faces then (as Gloria Swanson would say about silent movie stars in <u>Sunset Boulevard</u>), and they had wondrous nicknames for a boy to cherish

Notes:

and to remember – King Carl, Prince Hal, Big Poison, Little Poison, Dizzy, Daffy, The Bambino, The Yankee Clipper, The Thumper, The Wild Horse of the Osage. And Lefty as in Lefty O'Doul, which Arthur Brisbane, once the dean of lofty pundits, said was the most perfect name for baseball that there ever was.

They still play in my dreams on God's green in ballparks devoid of Astroturf, and they wear uniforms of a single color made out of flannel. I see them playing my dreams, all of these names from out of baseball's simpler, uncomputerized past, and I am playing with them.

Why am I telling you all this? Perhaps it is because I have been wondering if others, too, have the same baseball dreams. For after so many unrequited years, these dreams must surely be baseball's way of returning our love.

Lesson 5: READING RATES FOR COLLEGE: LIFE IN THE FAST LANE

Notes:

Reading Rates Chart — 1000 Work Article

MINUTES	WORD RATE PER MINUTE
1:00	1000
2:00	550
2:10	462
2:20	429
2:30	400
2:40	375
2:50	353
3:00	333
3:10	316
3:20	300
3:30	286
3:40	273
3:50	261
4:00	250
4:10	240
4:20	231
4:30	222
4:40	214
4:50	207
5:00	200
5:10	194
5:20	188
5:30	182
5:40	176
5:50	171
6:00	167
6:10	162
6:20	158
6:30	154
6:40	150
6:50	146
7:00	143

© 1988 by Cambridge Stratford, LTD.

Notes:

Comprehension Questions For "Baseball Dreams"

1. The author's hometeam was:

    a. Cards
    b. Pirates
    c. Cubs
    d. Giants

2. Baseball writers have done for this sport what Hemingway did for

    a. car racing
    b. bullfights
    c. tennis
    d. golf

3. The most perfect name in baseball was said to be
    a. Dizzy
    b. Daffy
    c. King Carl
    d. Lefty O'Doul

4. Early memories of baseball, according to the author, included

    a. radio descriptions
    b. real grass
    c. flannel uniforms
    d. all of the above

5. The author starred in high school games

    True or False

6. The word platitudinous means

    a. cheering
    b. commonplace
    c. unique
    d. wonderful

7. "There was larceny in my heart but my feet were honest" refers to
    a. stealing bases
    b. hitting the ball
    c. playing shortstop
    d. pitching the ball

8. The "Arkansas Hummingbird" was a Cubs pitcher.

    True or False

9. A capriciously feminine inspirer of futile fantasies means

    a. constant
    b. steady
    c. fickle
    d. resolute

10. The Yankees and the White Sox are National League teams.

    True or False

Lesson 5: READING RATES FOR COLLEGE: LIFE IN THE FAST LANE

Notes:

Answer Key

Speed Reading Comprehension Questions:

1. C   2. D   3. T   4. B   5. C
6. A   7. T   8. D   9. T   10. A

Column Reading

1. 250   2. 250   3. twice   4. practice   5. newspapers

Keyword Reading

1. learned person   2. 100   3. 230   4. three   5. 1985

Rapid Textbook Survey

1. Dealing With Delinquency: An Investigation of Juvenile Justice
2. yes   3. yes   4. legal options for dealilng with delinquents
5. 7   6. yes   7. 15 minutes

How Much Sleep Is Enough?

1. A   2. B   3. C   4. T   5. C

Baseball Dreams

1. C   2. B   3. D   4. D   5. F
6. B   7. A   8. T   9. C   10. F

Notes

References

Atkinson, Ronda H. and Debbie G. Longman. <u>Reading Enhancement and Development</u>. St. Paul, Minnesota: West Publishing Co., 1985, pp. 300-321.

Brown, James. <u>Reading Power</u>. Lexington, Mass.: D.C. Heath and Co., 1983, pp. 71-166.

Fry, Edward B. <u>Skimming and Scanning</u>. Providence, R.I.: Jamestown Publishers, 1978.

Heilman, Arthur W. <u>Improve Your Reading Ability</u>, Third Edition. Columbus, Ohio: Merrill Publishing Co., 1976, pp. 1-13, 45-52.

Joffe, Irwin L. <u>Opportunity for Skillful Reading</u>, Third Edition. Belmont, Calif.: Wadsworth Publishing Co., 1980, pp. 329-336.

Kollaritsch, Jane. <u>Reading and Study Organization Methods for Higher Learning</u>. Columbus, Ohio: Komo Associates, 1981, pp. 69-175.

McWhorter, Kathleen T. <u>College Reading and Study Skills</u>. Boston, Mass.: Little, Brown Co., 1986, pp. 295-319.

Smith, Samuel. <u>Read It Right and Remember What You Read</u>. New York, New York: Barnes and Noble, 1970.

Spargo, Edward and Glenn R. Williston, <u>Timed Readings</u>, Levels 1-8. Providence, Rhode Island: Jamestown Publishers, 1975.

Reading For Comprehension

**Lesson 6:
READING
FOR STUDY:
SLOW ME
DOWN, LORD!**

Objectives:

1. The student will recognize the need for several steps in reading a textbook for study purposes.

2. The student will be able to establish the optimum reading rate for study purposes.

3. The student will be able to state the steps used in the SQ3R Reading Method.

Notes:

SQ3R Worksheet For Textbook Study

Title of Textbook: _____

Estimated Time Needed for Chapter (from Chapter 5) _____

Questions from First Heading _____
_____
_____
_____
_____
_____

Important New Vocabulary _____
_____
_____

Major Concepts to Recall   1. _____
                            2. _____
                            3. _____

Questions from Second Heading _____
_____
_____
_____
_____
_____

Important New Vocabulary _____
_____
_____

Major Concepts to Recall   1. _____
                            2. _____
                            3. _____

ETC.

RECITE PROCESS

REVIEW PROCESS

Lesson 6: READING FOR STUDY: SLOW ME DOWN, LORD!

Notes:

From <u>Maternal Newborn Nursing: Care Of The Growing Family</u>, 2nd ed. by Adele Pillitteri. Publishers, Little Brown and Company.

5. Legal Aspects of Maternal-Newborn Nursing

As nursing becomes more complex, the legal responsibilities of nurses become more complex. Legal obligations must be considered.

Sources of Law

A law can be defined as a *man-made rule* that regulates human social conduct in a formally prescribed and legally binding manner. In the United States, laws are derived from two separate sources: statutory law and common law.

STATUTORY LAW

A statutory law is a *legislated law* or rule made by a governing body. It is equally binding on all citizens in that jurisdiction. Laws that set speed limits or prohibit robbery or littering are examples. Nurse practice acts, because they are formulated by state legislatures, are examples of legislative (statutory) laws pertinent to nursing.

COMMON LAW

Common law is a *judicial decision*. Legislative bodies cannot anticipate all the situations that can arise or all the different ways people will break laws. Thus, when a situation occurs that has never happened before (someone discovers how to transfer funds from other bank accounts to his bank account by computer), a judge examines the circumstances and makes a decision as to the nature of the act. He asks, if someone robs a bank by this method, is it the same as robbing a bank by showing a gun to a teller or is it different? Once a circumstance has been considered by a judge (that bank robbing is bank robbing no matter how it is done), there is a *precedent* as to the nature of that kind of act. When the same circumstances arise again, the second person will probably find himself held as liable as was the person who was involved when the precedent was set. Common law is often called the *law of precedents*.

Types of Law

In the United States there are two major divisions, or types, of law: criminal and civil law.

CRIMINAL LAW

A *crime* is an offense against the government or against society as a whole. A person who commits a crime has charges brought against him by the governing body. Embezzlement, murder, and forgery are examples of crimes. If a money penalty is involved as punishment, the money is paid to the governing body

Notes:

(paying a speeding ticket or paying a fine for embezzlement).

CIVIL LAW

A *civil offense* is an offense against an individual. If a money penalty is involved as punishment, the money is paid to the injured individual. Nurses may be guilty of either criminal or civil actions or both. Practicing without a nursing license, for example, is a crime or a criminal law offense. It is in violation of a state law; it has the potential of endangering a large number of people. Negligence and malpractice harm individuals; they are, therefore, civil offenses. Any money to be paid because of a negligence or malpractice suit is paid to the individual harmed by the error.

Negligence

All adults are responsible for conducting themselves at all times so as not to bring harm to others. Negligence is omitting to do something that a reasonable person would do under the same circumstances or doing something that a reasonable person under those circumstances would *not* do.

On a slippery, icy day, for example, the reasonable man shovels his front walk so that people, such as the mailman, who must walk on it will not slip and be injured. If a man did not shovel his walk and the mailman slipped, fell, and broke a leg, the man might be found guilty of negligence, or of not doing what the average person does.

Malpractice

Malpractice is professional negligence, either the omission of something that a reasonable nurse would do in the circumstances or the commission of something that a reasonable nurse would not do in those circumstances.

Taking vital signs frequently for the first hour following childbirth, for example, is an activity that the average nurse appreciates is important and does conscientiously. Not taking vital signs during that time could be interpreted as malpractice if injury happened to the patient during that time. The term *prudent* is often used in legal documents to denote reasonableness; legal phraseology considers what the prudent nurse would do.

Standards of Care

Whether a nurse has acted in a reasonable or prudent manner in a situation is often not an easy decision to make; in every situation there is always more than one way to do something. A number of sources are used to determine standards of nursing practice.

LEGISLATIVE SOURCES

Nurses are responsible for observing legislative law. The chief legislated laws that concern nurses are the nurse practice acts. You should be familiar with the wording of the Nurse Practice Act of your state so you can be certain that you are not only practicing within the scope of it but practicing to the full extent allowed by the Act. Nurses who take it upon themselves to make a medical diagnosis are at that point practicing medicine and functioning outside the standard level of nursing in the state.

COMMON LAW SOURCES

Common law sources are many. Which source would be used in any given instance depends on the circumstances and specific issues involved.

Health Agency Policies

You should be familiar with the policies and procedures of the health agency with which you work, as working in compliance with them is what the average nurse does. If a procedure is written poorly or wrongly, attempting to have it changed through the agency policy committee is more professional than just ignoring it. If the policies and procedures of an agency are such that you cannot work within them and still practice quality nursing, you will probably be wise to work elsewhere.

Job Descriptions

The average nurse works under the job description of her nursing position. If a job description is too limiting or "just not you," you are best advised to bend your efforts toward having the job description changed or obtaining a different position. It is difficult to justify performing functions outside your job description in the eyes of the law.

Voluntary Standards

Nursing organizations such as the National League of Nursing and the American Nurses' Association are concerned with setting practice standards. Standards for maternal-newborn nursing are discussed in Chap. 1. A nurse who does not meet these standards of care is not practicing at the level of the reasonable or average nurse.

Bills of Rights

The American Hospital Organization has devised a bill of rights for the hospitalized patient. Specialty

Lesson 6: READING FOR STUDY: SLOW ME DOWN, LORD!

Notes:

groups have listed rights for the handicapped, the child, and the mentally retarded. The Pregnant Patient's Bill of Rights is shown in Appendix A. Such a list of rights has implications in the determination of average practice standards.

Level of Knowledge

The more background and experience a nurse has, the higher the standard of care she is expected to provide. This places a responsibility on nurses to use all their knowledge every time they give patient care. For example, a new graduate would be expected to pick up changes on a fetal heart monitor strip when they first become evident. A nurse who has had experience working with fetal heart monitors or has taken an advanced course in fetal heart monitoring would be expected to pick up subtle changes even before they become truly definitive on the fetal monitor strip. This philosophy, that nurses must perform at the highest level they have attained, ensures patients the best care possible.

Average Practice Criteria

In order to lay a groundwork of what is average care, any nurse might be asked to come to court and testify on the standard level of care in her community or agency. In this role, she is called an expert witness. Expert witnesses are often asked to assess whether or not the nurse in question used suitable judgment in determining her course of action.

Fig. 5-1. A nurse owes a special duty of care to all patients, especially those who are not able to voice their concerns well. (Courtesy of the Department of Medical Photography, Children's Hospital, Buffalo, N.Y.)

It is assumed that nurses will use judgment in delivering nursing care. For example, a physician orders "vital signs [VS] every 15 minutes for 1 hour" for a woman who has just delivered a child. In actuality he means far more than that. He not only means that you should take vital signs but assumes that you will *compare* the present readings with those previously taken to see whether a descreasing or increasing trend is occurring, make a decision as to whether the readings are normal or not, record the readings so they become part of the permanent record, and, if they are abnormal, alert him to that. An expert witness might testify that the order, VS q15min for 1 hour, denotes all those activities, and not doing them all is not consistent with the standard of nursing care in that community.

Textbooks and Professional Journals

Nursing textbooks are compilations of nursing knowledge. If a textbook states that women in labor should be asked to void every 4 hours, for example, this becomes a standard for care in labor against which nursing actions and safe practice can be measured.

The Nurse-Patient Relationship

In the eyes of the law a nurse-patient relationship is a very special, binding one. A nurse owes a special duty of care to a patient over and above that duty she owes to other people, and she must continue to give care and guard the safety of the patient until she is relieved appropriately (Fig. 5-1).

Initiating a nurse-patient relationship involves no

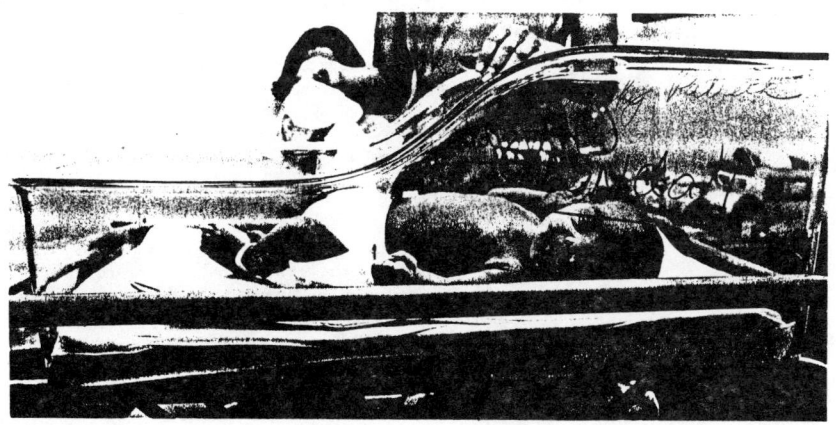

more action than beginning nursing care with that patient. No statement such as "Hello, I'm Miss Smith; I'm going to be your nurse for the day" is even necessary. Thus the relationship can be initiated as fully with an unconscious or anesthetized patient or a newborn who has no comprehension of legal aspects as with a legal-age consenting adult.

Whether a nurse-patient relationship exists or not has legal implications because of the special duty of care owed by a nurse to a patient.

ABANDONMENT

If a nurse initiates a nurse-patient relationship, she must maintain it until she is relieved appropriately. If you begin to care for a woman in labor, for example, then go to lunch without asking anyone to continue your care while you are gone and something detrimental happens during your unsupervised absence, you might be held liable for abandonment. A patient has the right to expect continuity of supervision from professional people whether you are physically present every minute or not.

In maternal-newborn nursing it is important to determine what procedures (abortion, perhaps) you ethically do not want to assist with. If you are asked to help with an abortion, for example, and you begin care, you must continue care until you are properly relieved despite any ethical conviction you have about assisting with abortions. The time to decide what you ethically want to do or not do is before your initiation of a nurse-patient relationship.

Criteria for Establishing Malpractice

In order for malpractice to be proved, three criteria must be present:

1. The nurse must have omitted doing something that a reasonable nurse would do under the circumstances or have done something that a reasonable nurse would not do under the circumstances.
2. Patient injury must have occurred.
3. There must be proximal cause between the action of the nurse and the injury.

For example, Mrs. K. has a urinary tract infection following delivery of her infant, and you are asked to administer ampicillin 250 mg to her. You make an error in calculating the dose and administer 500 mg of ampicillin instead. You have made an error; the first criterion is present. Because safe ampicillin doses vary widely, however, no harm occurs to the patient; the second criterion does not exist.

In another instance, a physician orders penicillin to be given to a woman in her sixth month of pregnancy to treat a urinary tract infection. You ask her whether she is allergic to penicillin and you check her records to see that she has no previous allergy to penicillin. A few minutes after you inject the medication, however, the woman becomes extremely short of breath and undergoes an anaphylactic reaction. This leads to a spontaneous abortion. The woman brings suit against you for administering an unsafe drug to her. Although there is patient injury and the administration of the drug led directly to the injury, because you did what the average nurse does before administering penicillin (asked about allergies, checked the chart for allergies) not all three of the criteria necessary for malpractice are present. It is very unlikely these circumstances would result in a successful legal action.

In a third example, you make an error and give an injection of ampicillin meant for Mrs. A. to Mrs. B. Although there was no medical reason for Mrs. B. to receive the ampicillin, ampicillin is not contraindicated during pregnancy so no harm results. A month later, the woman begins vaginal spotting and aborts. She brings suit against you for the medication error. Two criteria for malpractice are present: an error on your part and an injury (she has aborted). Since there is no proximal cause between an injection of ampicillin and abortion, however, the third criterion for malpractice is still not present.

RES IPSA LOQUITUR

Ordinarily, proving that a nurse has made an error is the responsibility of the patient. In certain instances, the proof of error is not difficult. If a patient should receive a burn on her arm, for example, in the shape of a heating pad after you applied such a pad to her arm, it is obvious that the burn resulted from the heating pad. *Res ipsa loquitur*, freely translated, is the Latin phrase for "the thing speaks for itself," or proof that an error has been made speaks for itself.

CONTRIBUTORY NEGLIGENCE

Contributory negligence occurs when a patient plays a part in his own injury. For example, you tell a woman after delivery of her baby that she should not get out of bed without your help because she will feel light-headed following her anesthetic. She ignores your instructions and walks to the bathroom by herself and falls and injures herself. She has contributed to her injury. Contributory negligence would not apply if at the time you gave the instruction she was too sleepy or in some other way could not understand or comprehend the importance of your message.

Lesson 6: READING FOR STUDY: SLOW ME DOWN, LORD!

Notes:

RESPONDEAT SUPERIOR
Every nurse is responsible for her own actions. She is also responsible for the personnel she supervises. As an everyday example of the application of this doctrine, if you take your car in to be repaired, you can expect to have it repaired at the level that you discuss with the owner of the repair shop, whether he actually repairs it or has a helper do it. If you are team leader and ask a practical nurse to pass medications for the day to help out (something ordinarily a registered nurse's duty) and she makes an error, you are responsible for her error by the doctrine of *respondeat superior* (literally, "let the master answer"). A patient has the right to expect that you will coordinate a level of care for him equal to that you would give yourself.

Incident Reports
One of the criteria for evaluating whether an action constitutes malpractice is whether you did what the average nurse would do *in those circumstances*. An incident report is your avenue to explain what the circumstances were. The three topics that you want to comment on are whether an error occurred or not, whether an injury occurred or not, and any connection between the two (proximal cause).

THE ERROR
State exactly what happened as you know it. You asked a woman her name to be certain that she was Mrs. Smith; she said yes. Unfortunately, there were two women in clinic named Mrs. Smith; you gave ampicillin to the wrong woman.

Incident reports are not the place for apologizing ("I'm sorry I did this but I learned a lot from it; I'll be a better nurse in the future"). In many states, incident reports are admissible evidence in court. It is a constitutional right that you do not have to testify against yourself. Self-incriminating statements on incident reports are a form of testifying against yourself.

Angry statements—"This is an example of why this policy is stupid"—are inappropriate on incident reports. They do not evidence sound thinking and they interfere with demonstrating that although you have made an error you are overall a responsible person.

THE INJURY
Some nurses are reluctant to describe a patient's injury thoroughly on a report because the description will reveal that an injury did indeed occur. In actuality, the description serves to show the limitation of the injury. A statement such as "There was an elevated, reddened area 2 cm by 1 cm on Mrs. J.'s right elbow after she fell, but she moved the joint readily without evidencing pain" shows that certainly the woman did bump her elbow when she fell. It also shows that the elbow must not have been broken; that is, it defines the extent of the injury.

THE PROXIMAL CAUSE
If you make an error in administering nursing care, it is imperative to include in your report the response of the patient to that error. If you gave an excessive dose of insulin to Mrs. J., who is pregnant and diabetic, for example, it would be important to document that, despite your error, at the time the insulin reached its maximum effect her blood sugar fell only to 80 mg per 100 ml. If her child is born later with a congenital anomaly, you have documented that, although you made an error, there is probably little connection between your error and the pregnancy's poor outcome.

Statute of Limitations
If you commit an error in nursing practice today, it is difficult to feel completely free of having a suit brought against you until it is no longer possible for a malpractice suit to be instituted against you. All states have statutes of limitations, or time spans, in which people can bring suit. After that period of time has passed, the threat of lawsuit is over. In most states the time span is three to five years. The exception is involved in the maternal-child health area of nursing. If parents choose not to bring a lawsuit against health personnel concerning a child's injury, there are instances in which the child was allowed to bring the suit himself when he reached legal age. This has implications for detailed charting. No one can remember what she did or what she was thinking three or five years ago, much less 20 years ago.

High-Risk Health Care Areas
All of maternal-newborn care is a high-risk area because you always care for two persons when you are caring for a pregnant woman; you care for individuals unable to protest or guide you into safe practice when you care for newborn infants. Within the maternal-newborn area some situations have higher risk for potential incidents than others. High-risk factors are:

New equipment (with which you are unfamiliar)
Electrical equipment (the possibility of burns or electrical shock always exists)

Legal Aspects of Maternal-Newborn Nursing 49

© 1988 by Cambridge Stratford, LTD.

Notes:

Medication (individual differences may affect safe dosage)

Heating and cooling devices (the possibility of burn always exists)

Controversial areas such as research or new procedures (misunderstandings of the procedure may result)

Emergency situations (action may be undertaken too swiftly, before all safety factors are considered)

NEW EQUIPMENT

Any time you are dealing with new equipment you must be certain that you thoroughly understand the purpose of the equipment and how to operate it. Ignorance, because you did not understand how to operate a piece of equipment, is no excuse for causing patient injury. Get proper instructions before beginning care.

ELECTRICAL EQUIPMENT

Electrical equipment is always a high-risk factor because of the inherent dangers of injury from electrical shock. Modern intensive care nurseries are built with a minimum of 12 electrical outlet plugs for each baby. This reflects, in a 30-bed nursery, 360 chances for electrical injury. It is a nursing responsibility to see that frayed or broken cords are not used, that outlets are not overloaded, and that electrical cords or plugs are not allowed to come in contact with water sources.

MEDICATIONS

Medicine giving is an area that is ripe for error due to the constantly increasing number of medicines for which a nurse is responsible. You have an added responsibility not to administer a drug that has teratogenic (capable of causing fetal injury) properties to pregnant women.

HEATING AND COOLING DEVICES

Whenever you work with equipment that has the potential to heat or cool, you are working with equipment that has the potential to burn. Postpartum women often have sitz baths, K-pads, or heat lamp treatments ordered for them to encourage perineal healing. Infants of low birth weight are often placed in incubators or under radiant heat sources or phototherapy lights. You must be aware of proper use of such equipment. Be meticulous about temperature settings, time limits, distance required, and specific precautions such as shielding the baby's eyes from phototherapy lights.

CONTROVERSIAL AREAS

In previous generations, childbearing was regarded as a process so unique that few interventions to interfere with or even assist it were attempted. Today, pregnancy may be initiated by artificial insemination; it may be ended by abortion. The fetus may be viewed by a fetoscope and even have a blood transfusion given to it in utero. Most of the controversy that arises over new procedures is concerned with ethical considerations, but there may be legal dimensions as well. Be certain that no procedure is carried out until informed consent has been obtained to ensure that there are no misunderstandings of the procedure later.

EMERGENCY SITUATIONS

In emergencies, steps of care must be taken quickly, but basic safety rules never change. A woman has the right to expect that additional complications will not happen to her due to someone's carelessness in an emergency situation.

Good Samaritan Laws

Many states have Good Samaritan laws or statutes that govern the actions of professional people in emergencies. Before Good Samaritan laws were passed, a nurse might have stopped at the scene of a car accident and found a pregnant woman bleeding heavily from a neck vein. She might have torn off the bottom of her skirt to make a compress to apply pressure to the wound. Later, after the woman was removed to the hospital, the wound site became infected and the woman developed septicemia and had an extended hospital stay. The woman might have initiated a lawsuit because a nurse should have known that with an open wound nothing but a sterile compress should have been applied.

In an emergency, perfect conditions, such as having a source of sterile compresses, do not apply. Good Samaritan laws state that the criterion against which a person in an emergency should be judged is not that of ideal conditions but what existed at the scene and time of the accident. In the example given, therefore, using a clean compress to halt extreme bleeding would be proper. If the nurse had used a greasy rag from the car trunk or had let the extreme bleeding go unchecked, then the care could be questioned.

The Suit-prone Nurse

Some nurses practice as if to attract lawsuits. People in general bring lawsuits against health personnel because they are unhappy with the quality or outcome of care. The concern or attitude of those who give that

Lesson 6: READING FOR STUDY: SLOW ME DOWN, LORD!

Notes:

care has a great deal to do with this unhappiness. A nurse who practices impersonally—not extending to women the courtesy of calling them by name or of remembering their names, not explaining procedures before they are carried out, not explaining what medications are being given and how they will work, not explaining what a woman can expect from a treatment or laboratory test—is asking for people to be unhappy with her. Obviously, a nurse who practices on the edge of safety—knowing a little but not a lot about the danger signs of pregnancy, the drugs she administers, or the equipment she works with—is a nurse who is suit-prone. More importantly, she is a poor model as a nurse.

The Suit-prone Patient

Pregnancy, labor and delivery, and the first days of the postpartum period are stressful. People under stress may not "hear" instructions given to them or may interpret them wrongly. During all phases of maternal-newborn nursing, therefore, instructions should be given with the appreciation that they are being offered to people under stress and that they may have to be repeated before they are comprehended. People under stress need support persons around them to serve as buffers. If they do not have them, they turn to health care personnel. If they do not receive support from health care personnel, they may turn to lawyers.

A major role of a nurse in maternal-newborn care is to serve as a supportive, concerned person for anyone who needs this type of interaction during a particularly important time.

A patient who understands what is going to happen to her because she has had adequate health teaching about pregnancy will not be surprised by what she is going through; she is less likely to be angry and upset because it is not a surprise. Health teaching, therefore, is a function of maternal-newborn nursing not only because not being surprised by events helps to encourage mother-infant bonding but also because it has legal aspects.

A woman who has a complication of pregnancy that results in death or morbidity of her infant loses a great deal. Sometimes she loses not only the child but future childbearing potential. A woman who is feeling loss is under enormous stress. She may seek a source of blame for what has happened to her. Unless she has very good explanations and feels trust and confidence in the people who care for her, she may bring a lawsuit. This type of lawsuit, initiated out of anger, helplessness, or a feeling of doing something even though it will not bring back the child, is generally groundless. It can be prevented if health care personnel appreciate what the loss of a child means to people and offer more constructive ways to deal with the frustration they face.

Informed Consent

In order for a person's signature on a consent form to be legal, the consent must be informed. That is, the person must be aware of what he is signing and understand the risks and expected outcome of the procedure and the risks and expected outcome if he does not consent to the procedure.

Many times you are asked to witness patients' signatures on consent forms. You must be certain that you are witnessing the signature of a person who has been informed, or you must have listened to the explanation of the procedure.

The term *informed* has special meaning for pregnant women in that the explanation must include not only any risk for the woman but risk for the fetus as well. If you did not hear the explanation or do not feel it was given accurately, you should not witness the form, or, if you witness it, you should add after your name, "witnessed signature only."

In many states, a pregnant teenager who is living away from home or is the parent of a child is considered an "emancipated minor." Although she cannot vote, an emancipated minor can sign consent for her own health care and that of her child. States have differing rules as to whether a teenager may sign consent for treatment for venereal disease or contraceptives. Federal law stipulates that a girl may consent to an abortion in early pregnancy without her parent's consent.

You should be familiar with the rules governing emancipated minors in your state. These rules are made because parents often do not accompany teenagers into health care facilities, and unless the minor's signature is accepted as legal in these instances, she would not be able to receive health care.

References

1. Bentz, J. M. Missed meanings in nurse-patient communications. *M.C.N.* 5:55, 1980.
2. Bernstein, A. H. Liability of hospitals—a continuing challenge. *Hospitals* 51:163, 1977.
3. Creighton, H. Legal concerns of nursing research. *Nurs. Res.* 26:337, 1977.
4. Creighton, H. Liability of a nurse for negligence. *Superv. Nurse* 9:53, 1978.

Notes:

5. Creighton, H. Slander. *Superv. Nurse* 9:64, 1978.
6. Creighton, H. More about informed consent. *Superv. Nurse* 9:84, 1978.
7. Fox, J. G., et al. Innovations in family and community health practice and the law. *Fam. Community Health* 1:19, 1978.
8. Hollowell, E. E. What every nurse should know about tort liability. *Hospitals* 51:97, 1977.
9. Hurt, T. The status of Good Samaritan statutes. *Health Educ.* 8:4, 1977.
10. Hysterectomies: Clinical necessity and consent. *Regan Rep. Nurs. Law* 18:2, 1977.
11. Kelly, L. S. The rights of young people in health care. *Nurse Pract.* 2:10, 1977.
12. Leitch, C. J., et al. A state by state report: The legal accommodation of nurses practicing expanded roles. *Nurse Pract.* 2:19, 1977.
13. Mancini, M. Nursing, minors and the law. *Am. J. Nurs.* 78:124, 1978.
14. Mumme, J. L. Seven surefire ways to lose a malpractice case. *R.N.* 40:60, 1977.
15. Newton, M., et al. Guidelines for handling drug errors. *Nursing 77* 7:62, 1977.
16. Nursing mistakes at patient's bedside: No M.D. liability. *Regan Rep. Nurs. Law* 17:2, 1977.
17. Paul, E. W., et al. Teenagers and pregnancy: The law in 1979. *Fam. Plann. Perspect.* 11:297, 1979.
18. Piazza, D. S., et al. Clinical nurse specialists: Issues, power and freedom. *Superv. Nurse* 9:47, 1978.
19. Rothman, D. A., et al. The nurse and informed consent. *J. Nurs. Adm.* 7:7, 1977.
20. Rozovsky, L. E. Answers to the 15 legal questions nurses usually ask. *Nursing 78* 8:73, 1978.
21. Sheffield, R. Complex medicolegal issues surround modern nursing practice. *Hospitals* 52:105, 1978.
22. Trendel-Korenchuk, D. M., et al. How state laws recognize advanced nursing practice. *Nurs. Outlook* 26:713, 1978.

52 *Maternal-Newborn Nursing*

Lesson 6: READING FOR STUDY: SLOW ME DOWN, LORD!

Notes:

THREE CRITERIA FOR ESTABLISHING MALPRACTICE

---

1. NURSE omitted something she should have done, or did something not reasonable to do under the circumstances.
2. PATIENT injury must have occurred.
3. CAUSE between action of the nurse and the injury.

Lesson 6: READING FOR STUDY: SLOW ME DOWN, LORD!

Notes:

Quiz

1. The two sources of law in the United States are _____ and _____ .

2. Nurses <u>may</u> be found guilty under two types of law, depending on the circumstances. They are _____ and _____ .

3. An example of negligence is _____ .

4. There are three criteria for establishing malpractice. They are:

    1. _____
    2. _____
    3. _____

5. Respondeat superior is Latin for _____ . and in nursing, it means a nurse is _____ .

Lesson 6: READING FOR STUDY: SLOW ME DOWN, LORD!

Notes:

Quiz Answers

1. The two sources of law in the United States are statutory and common;
2. Nurses may be found guilty under two types of law, depending on the circumstances. They are civil and criminal.
3. An example of negligence is not shoveling a slippery, icy sidewalk.
4. There are three criteria for establishing malpractice. They are: (1.) The nurse must have omitted doing something, or have done something which should not have been done; (2.) Patient injury must have occurred; (3.) There must be proximal cause between the action of the nurse and the injury.
5. Respondeat superior is Latin for "let the master answer," and in nursing, it means a nurse is responsible for the personnel she supervises.

Notes:

References

Atkinson, Ronda and Debbie Longman. Reading Enhancement and Development. St. Paul, Minnesota: West Publishing Co., 1985, pp. 40-77.

Joffe, Irwin L. Opportunity for Skillful Reading, Third Edition. Belmont California: Wadsworth Publishing Co., 1980, pp. 3-35.

Langan John. Reading and Study Skills, Third Edition. New York, New York: McGraw-Hill Co., 1986, pp. 194-211.

Maker, Janet and Minhette Lenier. College Reading, Book 2. Belmont, California: Wadsworth Publishing Co., 1982, pp. 86-107, 202-231, 332-356.

Pauk, Walter. How to Study in College, Second Edition. Boston, Massachusetts: Houghton Mifflin Co., 1974, pp. 140-152.

Vocabulary Building

**Lesson 7:
WORDS,
WORDS,
WORDS:
WHERE'S THE
ACTION?**

Objectives:

1. The student should be able to recognize the importance of vocabulary development for improved reading ability and the understanding of new concepts in college classes.

2. The student will be able to state at least five methods of learning new vocabulary.

3. The student should be able to identify the roots and affixes most frequently used in English words.

4. The student should be able to recognize the twenty words least apt to be known by college freshmen but most often used in college textbooks.

Notes:

Five Methods of Vocabulary Acquisition

1. SIGHT MEMORIZATION

   Examples: Salient – to project, to be outstanding
   – Big Nose
   Heuristic

2. PHONIC DETERMINATION

   Examples:

Spelling	Sounds Like	Means
Erudite	Air You Dite	Learned
Exacerbate	Eggs Ass Sir Bate	Make worse, irritate

3. CONTEXT

   Examples:

   1. Humor is <u>ubiquitous</u>; every culture on earth finds something funny.

      Humor is found <u>everywhere</u>. Something ubiquitous exists everywhere.

   2. The fight was so serious we thought Larry and Alan would never speak again, but Laurie was able to <u>ameliorate</u> the situation so everything turned out all right

   3. She was so obviously excited about seeing that movie that we <u>acquiesced</u> even though the reviews hadn't been very good.

   4. When Judy entered the room with Paul, Betsey whispered to Joan, "What he sees in her is <u>enigmatic</u> to me!"

4. PREFIXES

   ex-
   in-

   Roots

   Acri(mony)-
   Ten(acious)

   Suffixes

   mony-
   ate- abrogate, exacerbate

5. DICTIONARY/STUDY CARD METHOD - see examples

Lesson 7: WORDS, WORDS, WORDS: WHERE'S THE ACTION?

Notes:

Vocabulary Study Card Method

> **ABROGATE**
> 1. Did the court simply abrogate all responsibility for the act?
> 2. abrogare - to repeal - Latin
> 3. verb transitive (requires a direct objective)
> 4. to annul, to abolish, to nullify
> 5. ab' ro gat   AB row gate

Notes:

Vocabulary Study Card Method

ESOTERIC

1. The esoteric purposes of the club were only made clear upon initiation.
2. esoteros - inner - Greek
3. adjective
4. understood only by the inner circle or the initiated members of an organization.
5. es o ter/ ik   ess oh TEAR ik

Lesson 7: WORDS, WORDS, WORDS: WHERE'S THE ACTION?

Notes:

Twenty Words Needed (But Usually Not Known) by College Freshmen

Brief Meaning

1. ubiquitous _____
2. ameliorate _____
3. acrimony _____
4. enigmatic _____
5. abrogate _____
6. exacerbate _____
7. salient _____
8. acquiesce _____
9. capricious _____
10. specious _____
11. esoteric _____
12. erudite _____
13. tenacious _____
14. ambiguous _____
15. efficacious _____
16. anathema _____
17. aberrant _____
18. indigenous _____
19. heuristic _____
20. exigency _____

© 1988 by Cambridge Stratford, LTD.

Notes:

The Variable Story of the Car Accident

As told to your best friend:
_____
_____
_____
_____
_____
_____
_____
_____
_____
_____
_____

As told to your insurance agent:
_____
_____
_____
_____
_____
_____
_____
_____
_____
_____
_____

Changes Required:
_____
_____
_____
_____

Lesson 7: WORDS, WORDS, WORDS: WHERE'S THE ACTION?

Notes:

Summary Comments

Notes:

References

Lewis, Norman. Word Power Made Easy. New York, N.Y.: Doubleday Pocket Books, 1975.

Mathis, Phyllis. Increase Your Vocabulary. New York, N.Y.: Cambridge Book Company, 1976, pp. 1-30.

Paternoster, Lewis M. and Ruth L. Frager. 3 Dimensions of Vocabulary Growth. New York, N.Y.: Amsco College Publications, 1976, pp. 201-258.

Shepherd, James F. RSVP: The Houghton Mifflin Reading, Study and Vocabulary Program. Boston, Massachusetts: Houghton Mifflin Co., 1981, pp. 47-90.

Smith, Elliot L. Contemporary Vocabulary. New York, New York: St. Martin's Press, 1986.

Smith, S. Stephenson. How to Double Your Vocabulary. New York, New York: Funk and Wagnalls, 1974.

Listening Skills

Lesson 8: I CAN'T HEAR YOU: I'VE GOT MY HEADPHONES ON

Objectives:

1. The student will be able to recognize the difference between hearing a noise and actually listening to a sound.

2. The student will demonstrate the ability to listen and repeat information which is given by classmates.

3. Given a specific piece of knowledge, the student will be able to share this information with the class, and listen to make a decision about how the information relates to other facts presented by classmates.

Notes:

Listening Exercise:

DIRECTIONS SHEET

Write the directions to the Instructor's explanation of the passage that was recited in class about "Class Members Forming A Circle."

Write clearly so you could explain it to a classmate who may walk in the door within the next few minutes.

_____
_____
_____
_____
_____
_____
_____
_____
_____
_____
_____
_____
_____
_____
_____
_____
_____
_____
_____
_____
_____
_____

Lesson 8: I CAN'T HEAR YOU: I'VE GOT MY HEADPHONES ON

Notes:

Listening Exercise:

DIRECTION SHEET

Your group will be asked to form the circle described by the Instructor during the previous exercise.

After your group has completed the exercise, write down the names and the personality or physical traits which you heard.

NAMES:	TRAITS
1.	
2.	
3.	
4.	
5.	
6.	
7.	
8.	
9.	
10.	
11.	
12.	
13.	
14.	
15.	
16.	
17.	
18.	
19.	
20.	
21.	
22.	
23.	
24.	
25.	

© 1988 by Cambridge Stratford, LTD.

Notes:

Listening Exercise:

THE BANK ROBBERY MYSTERY

Following the description of a mystery, clues will be recited to help in solving it. Take notes about the clues to help in piecing the parts together to form your solution.

Characters in the Story _____
_____
_____
_____

Possible Motives _____
_____
_____
_____

Suspects _____
_____
_____
_____

Weapons _____
_____
_____
_____

Schedules _____
_____
_____
_____

Solution _____
_____
_____
_____

Answer _____
_____
_____
_____

Lesson 8: I CAN'T HEAR YOU: I'VE GOT MY HEADPHONES ON

Notes:

Summary Comments:

Notes:

References

Cohen, King, Knudsvigetal. Quest: Academic Skills Program. New York, New York: Harcourt Brace Jovanovich, Inc., 1973, pp. 88-152.

Pauk, Walter. How to Study in College. Boston, Massachusetts: Houghton Mifflin Co., 1974, pp. 125-139, 153-166.

Shepherd, James F. RSVP The Houghton Mifflin Reading, Study and Vocabulary Program. Boston, Massachusetts: Houghton Mifflin Co., 1981, pp. 211-289.

Woods, Nancy V. College Reading and Study Skills. New York, New York: Holt, Rinehart and Winston, 1986, pp. 31-48.

Yates, Virginia. Listening and Note-Taking. New York, New York McGraw Hill, 1979. (Tapes and Manuscripts)

Note Taking/Outlining

**Lesson 9:
MUSIC TO
YOUR EARS:
LECTURE
NOTES**

Objectives:

1. The student should exhibit the ability to produce two pages of clear, neat, useful notes for study.

2. The student should be able to list at least five direction words which guide our listening.

3. The student should be able to take notes using the method taught, and be able to produce study materials from the notes.

Lesson 9: MUSIC TO YOUR EARS: LECTURE NOTES

Notes:

	Note Paper
○	
○	
○	

© 1988 by Cambridge Stratford, LTD.

Lesson 9: MUSIC TO YOUR EARS: LECTURE NOTES

Notes:

Note Paper

Lesson 9: MUSIC TO YOUR EARS: LECTURE NOTES

Notes:

Note Paper

Lesson 9: MUSIC TO YOUR EARS: LECTURE NOTES

Notes:

Note Paper

Notes:

A Checklist For Note Taking Skills

Directions: Look at the set of notes you took and check yourself on the following areas:

The Notes I Took Include: Yes   No

The title, the lecturer's name, my name, the date

Clear headings and subheadings for topics

Underlined important words and phrases

Key points are numbered

Easily identifiable abbreviations/symbols

Study words in the left margin

All the important points in the lecture

No repetitions of material

Space to add missed material

Writing on only one side of the paper

Lesson 9: MUSIC TO YOUR EARS: LECTURE NOTES

Notes:

Seven Ways To Improve Your Concentration In Class

1. Do not sit near your best friend or your boy friend or girl friend in class. It is too easy to be distracted if you are not concentrating on the class but are, instead, whispering, passing notes, or exchanging glances and grimaces.

2. Sit away from the windows in a classroom. If a lecture becomes even slightly tedious, windows can be a strong distraction, for you will find yourself gazing out the window and daydreaming.

3. Instead, sit near the middle and front of the classroom. Most instructors of classes will speak most frequently to that section of the room. You will enable yourself to hear the lecture from that vantage point, and you will be able to see any diagrams, problems, etc., which are written on the blackboard.

4. Before attending classes, be sure you have eaten the appropriate meal. Hunger can, and does, distract attention, and a growling stomach distracts your classmates, too.

5. Dress comfortably for class. Fashion is definitely important on a college campus, but don't let yourself become so slavish to fashion that you aren't being practical. Classrooms can be too hot or too cold. You should be prepared for this, **and** you should wear clothes that are comfortable. It is difficult to concentrate on class lectures when all you can think of is your shoes are too tight!

6. Use the bathroom before you go to class. College professors do not expect to have students wandering in and out of class during a lecture or activity, and you cannot concentrate on note taking if you are uncomfortable.

7. Smile and nod occasionally at your professor. This usually will attract the speaker so he/she will begin to look at you more frequently. This eye contact helps you pay attention, and if you don't understand something, the instructor may notice that and repeat things until he/she is certain **you** understand! It also helps you to keep your mind from wandering in class.

Notes:

Note Taking Techniques

1. PAPER _____

_____

_____

_____

_____

_____

_____

2. SPACING AND INDENTATION _____

_____

_____

_____

_____

_____

_____

_____

3. ORGANIZATION _____

_____

_____

_____

_____

_____

_____

_____

4. FOLLOW-UP ACTIVITIES _____

_____

_____

_____

_____

_____

_____

_____

Lesson 9: MUSIC TO YOUR EARS: LECTURE NOTES

Notes:

Model Set of Notes:

JUDY STUDENT OCTOBER 25, 19 ____
HISTORY 101 DRS. O'CONNOR & McGLEN

WOMEN'S RIGHTS

1848 Seneca Falls	First major step toward female equality
1848 – Women's Rights Convention – Seneca Falls, NY
Stanton & Mott	Leaders – Elizabeth Cady Stanton
Lucretia Mott
Dec. of Sentiments	Produced the Declaration of Sentiments modeled after Declaration of Independence. DS & additional resolutions wanted:
1. end to discrimination against women in legal, economic and social issues
2. to express dissatisfaction with moral codes, divorce & criminal laws, & limited opportunities in education, church, & careers (especially medicine, law, and politics)
3 points of activity	Three high points of activity in women's movement
 1. 1848-1875   early period
 2. 1890-1925   suffrage
 3. 1966-present

Discrimination is deterrent to political activity
 1. cultural stereotypes about female abilities and the appropriate position of women in politics
 2. lack of preparation for political activity
 3. discrimination of male politicians reluctant to share power

(all three least strong w/young, college-educated woman, strongest w/elderly, poorly-educated, southerners) |

9.1

JUDY STUDENT OCTOBER 25, 19 ____
HISTORY 101 DRS. O'CONNOR & McGLEN
PAGE 2

VOTING

Considered the most basic form of citizen participation
1980 – 59.1% of men and 59.4% of women voted

1920	Women first allowed to vote in 1920 BUT:
4 Reasons why some women did not use the vote in the early years	1. voting made difficult when possible. Poll taxes, literacy tests, complex registration procedures used to prevent women (and blacks) from using their vote.
2. societal (cultural) pressures a problem. Ex. southern men and women more conservative, older, ethnic, immigrants reluctant (not as big a problem since the 1950s)
3. role conflict between motherhood & voting difficulty getting to the polls
4. lack preparation
    women unfamiliar with political procedures
    women unfamiliar with candidates & issues

Overcome by
 1. Formation of League of Women Voters
    – to educate women in political process
 2. Depression of 1930s
    – women voted in 1932 to change gov't.

Summary: By 1980, most barriers to women were eliminated |

9.2

© 1988 by Cambridge Stratford, LTD.

Notes:

References

Casey, Robert S. <u>Oral Communication</u>. New York, New York: Reinhold Book Division, 1958, pp. 32-149.

Malmber, Bertil. <u>Phonetics</u>. New York, New York: Dover Publications, Inc., 1963.

Nordberg H. Orville, Iris E. Nordberg, and Henry A. Bamman. <u>World of Words</u>. San Francisco, Calif.: Field Educational Publications, Inc. 1970.

Staton, Thomas F. and Emma D. Staton. <u>How to Study</u>, Seventh Edition. Nashville, Tennessee: How to Study. 1977, pp. 69-74.

Test Taking

Lesson 10:
YOU WANT ME TO DO WHAT? TAKE A TEST?

Objectives:

1. The student should be able to recognize at least five different types of test questions which may appear on college exams.

2. The student will determine how to maximize his/her chances of choosing the correct answer on a multiple choice exam.

3. The student should be able to recognize the differences among terms used in essay questions on an exam, and determine how to answer the question.

Notes:

Lesson 10 – Exams
PREPARATION:

1. Review underlined sections of textbook

2. Review lecture notes - key words

3. Review study cards

TYPES OF QUESTIONS

1. Multiple Choice

2. Fill-in-the-Blank

3. True/False

4. Matching

5. Sentence Completion

6. Essay Questions

TERMS MOST FREQUENTLY USED

1. Compare

2. Contrast

3. Describe

4. Prove

5. Review

6. Trace

Lesson 10: YOU WANT ME TO DO WHAT? TAKE A TEST? 107

Notes:

Possible Exam Questions

Objective: _____

_____

Essay: _____

_____

Notes:

Time Management for Exams

An exam begins at 10:00 a.m. The instructor has indicated that you have fifty (50) minutes for the exam. You spend five (5) minutes reading through the exam and checking the value of questions. You want to save at least five (5) minutes at the end so you can check your answers.

The exam has fifty (50) objective questions with one (1) point each and two (2) essay questions worth twenty-five (25) points each.

How will you plan your time?

10:00 a.m. – Begin Exam

_____
_____
_____
_____
_____
_____
_____
_____
_____
_____
_____
_____
_____
_____
_____
_____
_____

10:50 – Submit Paper - Exam Ends

Lesson 10: YOU WANT ME TO DO WHAT? TAKE A TEST?

Notes:

Can You Follow the Directions On a Test?

1. Read everything before you do anything.
2. Put your name in the top left corner of this page.
3. Draw three triangles after this sentence.
4. Put a circle around each triangle.
5. In the top right corner, write the name of your college.
6. In the bottom left corner of this page, draw four boxes.
7. In each box, put the name of your instructor.
8. Circle the word "boxes" in number 6.
9. If you are the first person to reach this number, call out loudly: "I am number one!"
10. Go back and do just number two.

© 1988 by Cambridge Stratford, LTD.

Notes:

Study Skills Post-Test

Part I: Multiple Choice: Choose the one option which is NOT CORRECT in the following statements.

1. On a four-point scale, a person who receives a grade of:

    a. "B" in a 3-hour course gets 9 quality points
    b. "C" in a 2-hour course gets 4 quality points
    c. "F" in a 3-hour course gets 3 quality points
    d. "A" in a 2-hour course gets 8 quality points

2. For effective study, a good student should know

    a. the number of hours he should plan to study
    b. that there are three types of objective test questions
    c. how to use at least three rates of reading
    d. five methods for learning new words

Part II. True or False – Circle your Answer.

3. A student taking fifteen credit hours should plan to spend a minimum of twenty hours a week on study.   True   False

4. The best place to sit in a lecture classroom is in the middle and toward the front.   True   False

5. Key words are useful for study when written in the margin of a notebook.   True   False

6. A "trace" question might be found on a history exam.   True   False

7. Intelligent students don't need a study system.   True   False

Lesson 10: YOU WANT ME TO DO WHAT? TAKE A TEST?

Notes:

Part III. Matching Question: Choose the answer in Column B which best fits the letter in Column A and enter the answer on the line.

Column A   Column B

a. ways in which we comprehend our reading   _____ 8. 3

b. words per minute Americans read   _____ 9. 120

c. "tri" is a word root which means   _____ 10. 30 (days)

d. class notes should be taken on _____ side(s) of the paper   _____ 11. 2

                                                                 _____ 12. 4

e. the typical number of credit hours needed for a bachelor's degree   _____ 13. 250

f. mnemonic device   _____ 14. 1

g. "recite" is the # _____ "R" in SQ3R

Part IV. Fill in the blank or complete the sentence.

15. An example of a "direction" word a student should listen for in a lecture is: _____ .

16. and 17. To really learn something, we must go through five steps. They are:

    1. motivation   2. selection   3. _____

    4. _____   5. review

18., 19. and 20. Watching someone do something is one way in which we learn. Three other ways are:

    a. _____

    b. _____

    c. _____

ANSWER KEY:

1. (c) 2. (d) 3. (F) 4. (T) 5. (T) 6. (T) 7. (F) 8. (c)
9. (e) 10. (F) 11. (g) 12. (a) 13. (b) 14. (d)
15. (subsequently, etc.) 16. (clarification) 17. (association)
18. (reading about it) 19. (listening to something)
20. (doing it or writing it down)

© 1988 by Cambridge Stratford, LTD.

Notes:

References

Test-Taking Skills: How to Succeed on Standardized Examinations, Part 1 and 2. White Plains, N.Y.: The Center for the Humanities, Inc.

Pauk, Walter. How to Study in College. Boston, Massachusetts: Houghton Mifflin Co., 1974, pp. 177-185.

Staton, Thomas F. and Emma D. Staton. How to Study, Seventh Edition. Nashville, Tennessee: How to Study, 1977, pp. 75-79.

Notes:

And, finally –

Completion of this course has given you a foundation on which to build your college career. Do not believe, however, that this will be <u>all</u> that is needed. After a few weeks in college you may find that you need more help. Every college provides services for students who are experiencing academic, personal, or financial difficulties. Seek out these resources.

Going to college can be scary and it can be exciting. It requires much more academic independence than most students have had to exhibit in the past. You should enjoy your college years, but you should also remember that the <u>academic</u> transcript will be the written document of your college career. Good study skills can make the transcript a permanent record of which you (and your family) can be proud. Keep this student workbook with you at college, and refer to it often. Review is the key to remembering, and this is true of study skills techniques, too!

Good luck and best wishes for a successful college career.

June Crawford

EVALUATION

We hope that you have benefited from your experience with <u>TEN TIPS FOR ACADEMIC SUCCESS</u>. We would like to learn about your experience so that we may continually improve upon our efforts to make this a better book for future users.

Please take a moment to offer your comments. Thank you.

Your School _____

City/State _____

My overall assessment was: ____ excellent ____ good ____ fair ____ poor

What I liked most about <u>TEN TIPS FOR ACADEMIC SUCCESS</u> was _____

_____

_____

What I liked least about <u>TEN TIPS FOR ACADEMIC SUCCESS</u> was _____

_____

_____

I (would, would not) recomment <u>TEN TIPS FOR ACADEMIC SUCCESS</u> for college bound students because _____

_____

_____

We would like to receive any other comments you would like to share. Thank you in advance!

June Crawford
June Crawford

OPTIONAL COMMENTS FOR PUBLICATION:

Please print or type your comments below for inclusion in future descriptions of <u>TEN TIPS FOR ACADEMIC SUCCESS.</u>

Your Name _____ Status: Student ___ Teacher ___ Other ___

Address _____

·· **FOLD HERE** ··

Comment: _____
_____
_____
_____
_____

Would you like to receive more information about other editions of The Cambridge-Stratford Study Skills Course (20 hr. – 6th-8th grades, 30 hr. – 9th-11th grades), <u>The Library Experience: Sharing The Responsibility</u> (5th-8th grades)?

Name _____

Address _____
_____

·· **FOLD HERE** ··

CUT PAGE OUT

NO POSTAGE
NECESSARY
IF MAILED
IN THE
UNITED STATES

BUSINESS REPLY MAIL
FIRST CLASS   PERMIT NO. 88   BUFFALO, N.Y.

Postage Will Be Paid By Addressee

CAMBRIDGE-STRATFORD
STUDY SKILLS COURSE
8560 Main Street
Harris Hill Square
Williamsville, New York 14221